THE FOUNTAINWELL DRAMA TEXTS

General Editors

T. A. DUNN

ANDREW GURR

JOHN HORDEN

A. NORMAN JEFFARES

R. L. C. LORIMER

BRIAN W. M. SCOBIE

14

HENRY FIELDING

TOM THUMB
and
THE TRAGEDY OF TRAGEDIES

Edited by

L. J. MORRISSEY

UNIVERSITY OF CALIFORNIA PRESS
Berkeley and Los Angeles · 1970

University of California Press
Berkeley and Los Angeles, California

First Published 1970
SBN: 520—01652–1 (cloth)
SBN: 520—01654–8 (paper)
Library of Congress Catalog Card No.: 75–92675

Originally published by Oliver and Boyd
Edinburgh, Scotland

Printed in Great Britain

ACKNOWLEDGMENTS

The editing of this play was made incomparably easier by the careful work of an earlier scholar, J. T. Hillhouse. Professor C. L. Murison of the Department of Classics, University of Western Ontario, was also most helpful with the translations in this play. Mr. John Horden of the University of Leeds was also a superbly patient and careful Textual General Editor.

L. J. M.

London, Ontario
1968

CONTENTS

CRITICAL INTRODUCTION

In 1730 Henry Fielding had four plays produced: *The Temple Beau* at Goodman's Fields, *The Author's Farce; And The Pleasures of the Town*, *Tom Thumb*, and *Rape upon Rape; or, The Justice Caught in his Own Trap* all at the Little Theatre in the Haymarket. In several ways this first year[1] of substantial dramatic production for Fielding is an epitome of his dramatic career. *Rape upon Rape* imitates a multiple-plot Jacobean comedy, full of blustering humorous characters. *The Temple Beau* is on a tried Restoration pattern. A young and clever rake succeeds in getting money from an old and difficult father, and there is the spice of the love pursuit for good measure. Two of the plays, however, are not imitations, although both are slightly derivative. *The Author's Farce* and *Tom Thumb*, two farce satires, show Fielding's independent ability. Both plays are distinctly *satura*, that is *potpourri*, *mélanges*, salads. Fielding's most exciting and most successful plays financially are all almost plotless salads in which songs, dances, verbal parody, and vignette scenes, attacking corrupt politicians or stupid theatre managers or obtuse physicians, are jumbled together. He not only opened but he ended his career with just such *satura*.

Pasquin. A Dramatic Satire on the Times: Being the Rehearsal of Two Plays, viz. A Comedy call'd, The Election; and a Tragedy call'd, The Life and Death of Common-Sense (1736), which attacks Fielding's two continuing enemies—bad theatre and corrupt government, and *The Historical Register, For the Year 1736* (1737), which continues this attack, were so sharp that they were instrumental in bringing about the Licensing Act,[2] urged through the House of Commons by the Walpole ministry in May of 1737. Both of these *mélanges* are held together by the imposed form of a rehearsal. In each play the author is present to run through the play with the cast; and friends of the

[1] His first play, *Love in Several Masques*, had been produced in February of 1728, just a month before he registered for his year and a half at the University of Leyden.

[2] The Act virtually limited production of legitimate drama to the two patent houses, Theatre Royal, Drury Lane and the Theatre Royal in Covent Garden. It also placed the licensing of new plays under the Lord Chamberlain, giving him much more power than he formerly had.

author, or people he wants to please, with names like Sneerwell and Sowrwit, sit by and make comments. Fielding had used a modified version of this same form in *The Author's Farce*. Here, Luckless, the poet, becomes master of his puppet show, *The Pleasures of the Town*, which is presented within a conventional love plot, set in Grub Street. Fielding probably got the idea for this play within a play, or more specifically for this rehearsal within a play, from George Villier's (Duke of Buckingham) *The Rehearsal* (1671). After Fielding, this form nearly becomes a tradition in dramatic burlesque. Sheridan used it in *The Critic* (1779), and a minor dramatist like David Garrick used it in *Peep behind the Curtain* (1767). In his two later plays, Fielding employed the form for considerably more then dramatic burlesque. He used it for political satire so vigorous that the thick-skinned Sir Robert Walpole saw to it that Fielding's Little Theatre in the Haymarket was closed three days after the Licensing Act became law on 21 Jun. 1737.

The productions of his first year, then, epitomise his career because they show him both as imitator and as imaginative innovator, particularly in satire. But Fielding's first real year in the theatre is significant for another reason.

Three of his four plays in 1730 were produced in the Little Theatre in the Haymarket. While Fielding had plays produced by the more seasoned company at the patent theatre in Drury Lane, particularly from 1732 until about 1735, he inevitably fell back on the Little Theatre in the Haymarket to produce his political satires when they were refused production by the management of Drury Lane or another larger theatre. *Don Quixote in England* (1734) is an example, *Pasquin* another. One of the reasons for his move to Drury Lane in 1732 was the banning of *The Grub-Street Opera* (see *The Daily Post*, 14 Jun. 1731) by the Lord Chamberlain and the subsequent harassment that in effect closed the company in June of 1731. The theatre remained closed until February of 1732. Finally, in 1736 Fielding found it necessary to assume the management of the Little Theatre, to re-assemble a company of players and to produce his most virulent satires himself.

Between 1730 and 1732 three of Fielding's best farce burlesques were produced, or prepared for production: *Tom Thumb* (1730), later turned into *The Tragedy of Tragedies* (1731); *The Grub-Street Opera* (1731), suppressed by the Lord Chamberlain; and *The Covent-*

Garden Tragedy (1732). These three plays did not make use of the rehearsal or play within a play convention. Instead, in two of the plays Fielding parodied legitimate dramatic forms and in one he used a newer burlesque convention.

The Covent-Garden Tragedy is a bawdy blank verse parody of the neo-classical tragedy then becoming popular with the production of plays like Addison's *Cato* (1713), Ambrose Philips' *The Distrest Mother* (1712), and James Thomson's *The Tragedy of Sophonisba* (1730). It is set not in Rome, or some part of the Empire, but in an eighteenth-century house of prostitution run by Mother Punchbowl. Both the situation and the bathos of the verse are an attack on this form. To continue a tradition which he began with *Tom Thumb*, Fielding added a learned Prolegomena to the printed play, in which he is able to attack his critics on *The Grub-Street Journal*. With this play, Fielding seems to have lost interest in political satire, probably because of the furor that *The Grub-Street Opera* had caused a year earlier.

In *The Grub-Street Opera* Fielding simply used a dramatic vehicle already established by Gay as a means of burlesquing opera while at the same time satirising the contemporary political situation. This delightful ballad opera, written by "Scriblerus Secundus", and full of excellent songs like "The Roast beef of England" and "A Pipe of Tobacco", is a sharp satiric attack on the Walpole ministry and on the court of George II. Sir Robert Walpole is Robin, the butler in a Welsh household where Lady Apshinken (Queen Caroline) rules her epicurean husband, and where their sexually inadequate son, Master Owen (the Prince of Wales) pursues the chamber maids. The satire is so open that it is no wonder that Walpole saw to it that the play was suppressed.

Tom Thumb was Fielding's first overwhelming success. It ran nearly uninterrupted at the Little Theatre from Friday 24 Apr. until Monday 22 Jun., nearly forty nights.[3] And it ran to over-flowing and sophisticated houses night after night. "So great was the demand for seats from 'persons of quality' within a week or two that it was necessary

[3] During most of this run, it was an afterpiece to Fielding's *The Author's Farce*, although during the early part of the run (27 Apr. and 29 Apr.) they had attempted to join it with a farcical ballad opera called *The Female Parson; or, Beau in the Suds*. Only one night early in the run was *Tom Thumb* not played at all (30 Apr.).

to put pit and boxes together in order to accommodate them."[4] This success can be accounted for in part by the vigour and gaiety of the farce, but it is the satire and the burlesque that must have pleased Fielding's audience most.

The parody of heroic drama, and theatrical bombast in general, is delicious. As F. Homes Dudden points out,[5] it has its superhuman hero, the conqueror of giants, only he is bathetically reduced in size to a pigmy. It has the love and jealousy so necessary to a heroic plot. Tom and Huncamunca love each other, but the Queen too loves Tom, and so conspires with Grizzle. It also has a perfect bit of heroic farce action in the last act when Thumb's spirit comes back to haunt the Court. Grizzle simply runs Tom's ghost through, and the essential revenge plot comes to a happy conclusion. Then too, the whole play, or much of it, was merely a patchwork of lines from earlier heroic or bombastic plays. Fielding mercilessly searched everyone from John Fletcher to John Dryden and James Thomson for their weakest and most absurd lines and wove them together to make his scenes. The nicest instance of this is his ruthless quoting of John Gay, both when Gay is attempting to write a tragedy (*The Captives*) in the high style, and when he is burlesquing such tragedy (*The What D'Ye Call It*). Besides this literary burlesque, the play makes some perfect hits on Fielding's life-long enemies, the tribe of physicians.

It seems unlikely, however, that the play was successful as a result of its verve or its burlesque alone. *The Covent-Garden Tragedy*, although bawdier and not quite as good, has both; and it ran as an after-piece for only two or three nights in June of 1732. It must have been its satire that kept this little play running. Even though the Earl of Egmont's opening night diary entry does not indicate that he was aware of political satire in the play,[6] there were references to Walpole and the Court throughout that the audience would probably have identified, thus doubling their pleasure. There are references to fox-hunting, Walpole's favourite pastime, and to peace and safety, the mainstay of Walpole's foreign policy; the Queen favours Thumb, the "Preserver of [the] Kingdom", as Caroline favoured Walpole.

A few weeks after the play was first produced and printed (it was sold at the theatre on opening night), it underwent its first revision.

[4] Wilbur Cross, *The History of Henry Fielding*, I, p. 88.

[5] *Henry Fielding His Life, Works, and Times*, I, p. 62.

[6] *The Diary of the Earl of Egmont*, I (H.M.C., No. 63, 1920), p. 97.

The two bailiff scenes were added to the text, increasing the honour of the fiery-tempered hero and probably suggesting Walpole's trouble with the city merchants. A single additional speech was given to the King at the end of II. VIII, where his maggot simile might be a nasty new thrust at Walpole. Preface, epilogue, and prologue were also added. These were designed to ridicule the failure of literary common sense, with Colley Cibber as the particular butt. Actor, manager of Drury Lane, and poet-playwright, Cibber was about to "Out-do his usual Out-doing" and become Poet Laureate (3 Dec. 1730). In anticipation of this event, Fielding made Cibber the chief fool of his Preface. Later, Fielding even added, or allowed Thomas Cooke to add, several new scenes to *Tom Thumb* while it was being produced in Nov. 1730 and just before Cibber was made Laureate. The new scenes called *The Battle of the Poets; or, The Contention for the Laurel* pit Fopling Fribble (Cibber had won his reputation as an actor playing the part of Lord Foppington in Vanbrugh's *The Relapse*) against several other identifiable hack poets of the day. Cibber is finally awarded the laurel and a mug of ale for his extemporaneous verse.

The revised play was attributed to "Scriblerus Secundus". This is obviously Fielding's attempt to associate himself with the group of Tory wits who had banded together in 1713 to form "The Scriblerus Club". Swift, Gay, Pope, Parnell, and Queen Anne's physician, Dr Arbuthnot, had met and conceived a massive burlesque of the various kinds of pedantry and bad writing of their day. This burlesque was to be called *The Memoirs of Martinus Scriblerus*. While the fragmentary *Memoirs* were not published until 1741, some of the greatest English satire developed out of this specific burlesque intention. *Gulliver's Travels* (1726), *The Beggar's Opera* (1728), and *The Dunciad* (1728) were all, in part, a result of the club. Although the Scriblerus project had long been abandoned by its originators when Fielding took it up in 1730, Pope continued to be interested in it and probably thought of this project to burlesque pedantry, under the pseudonym of Scriblerus, as the exclusive right of members of the club. So, instead of admitting Fielding to the group of young wits that hovered about him in 1730, Pope countenanced the barrage of criticism that *The Grub-Street Journal* began to direct at Fielding after *Tom Thumb*.

On 24 Mar. 1731 Fielding brought out a much revised version of the play, now called *The Tragedy of Tragedies; or The Life and Death of*

Tom Thumb the Great, which ran steadily through April and intermittently through May of 1731.[7] In this new play the political satire is even clearer. Thumb is referred to as "the Great"; Walpole was now constantly referred to in pamphlets as the Great man. An open battle takes place between Grizzle and Thumb over love at Court. Walpole and Townshend had recently quarrelled, Townshend leaving the ministry and breaking his long association with Walpole. The quarrel had been occasioned, in large part, by Walpole's handling of the Treaty of Seville, arranged with the strong support of the Queen of Spain, who may be represented in *The Tragedy of Tragedies* by the new character, Glumdalca, the giant Queen.

The added character, Glumdalca, also allows Fielding to heighten his parody of heroic drama. Now the interlocking love and honour complications become incredibly, heroically confused. Tom is loved by Huncamunca, by the Queen, Dollallolla, and by the giant Queen, Glumdalca. Huncamunca also loves Grizzle. And the King loves both his Queen and Glumdalca. Fielding is also able to introduce a fine heroic battle with drums, armies, trumpets, thunder and lightning.

Bad or bombastic drama is not the only thing to suffer in this revised play. Cibber is dropped as the fool, and a pedantic scholar, called H. Scriblerus Secundus, is substituted. With this device, Fielding is able to sharpen his literary satire by quoting the lines specifically used or parodied[8] at the same time that he attacks the dullness of literary scholarship and wrong-headed criticism. Classical scholars like Bentley, Wotton, Scaliger and Pieter Burmann, under whom Fielding apparently suffered at Leyden, are attacked for their pedantry, and critics like Dennis for their shouted literal-minded assertions and their defence of sublime enthusiasm. In his preface and footnotes Scriblerus

[7] *The Tragedy of Tragedies* was the main offering during most of its run, being played together with Fielding's *The Letter Writers*, *The Author's Farce*, and, most often, with *The Welch Opera*. Only once during its initial run was it an afterpiece: on 5 May, near the end of its run, it was played as an afterpiece with *The Orphan* at Henry Gifford's theatre in Goodman's Fields.

[8] J. T. Hillhouse in his edition of *The Tragedy of Tragedies* points out that Fielding "burlesqued directly in *The Tragedy of Tragedies* . . . at least forty-two" plays, not counting the unidentified lines from Shakespeare and one line from his own *Coffee House Politician*. Dryden, Lee, and Banks were most often parodied because they were the principal writers of heroic tragedy. Although few playwrights in Fiedling's day wrote in this genre, heroic tragedies were often acted.

offers learned disquisitions on dating, attribution and sources of the text (PREFACE), on giants (I. I.*d*) and on proverbial wisdom (II. X.†). He offers emendations and variant readings (I. I.*c*). He argues with mock commentators (I. I.*h* and I. II.*p*). In short, Fielding creates a little mock scholarly storm, complete with Latin quotations and counter-quotations, and corrections in the reading of Aristotle (PREFACE). As a kind of classical example of the mindless pedantry Fielding is attacking, Scriblerus' footnote comment on the line "Ah wretched Queen!" (II. VIII) juxtaposes lines from weak bombastic plays by Edward Young and David Mallet with lines from Seneca, a tale by Herodotus, and an essay by Montaigne, as though they were of equal value. For Scriblerus, footnotes grow on footnotes; one speech in a play by Dryden is made into two footnotes (II. X.*u* and *x*).

Fielding's specific humour in the play varies from jokes about Dennis (II. IV.*n*), to doggerel rhyme (*drunk ha* with *Huncamunca* and *fine is* with *Highness*), and doggerel metre. The play is full of bathetic reduction—"I feel Death rumbling in my Brains" (III. IX. 33) or "With those last Words he vomited his Soul" (III. IX. 43)—and finely turned comic tropes (III. II. 13 or 44). The action itself, of course, is excellent farce.

Undoubtedly Fielding got his idea for a pedantically footnoted and prefaced text from Pope and Swift. This Scriblerian technique had been employed by Swift in the 1710 edition of *A Tale of a Tub*. Swift had in turn inspired *A Comment upon the History of Tom Thumb* (1711) by William Wagstaff, which is completely annotated and with which Fielding might have been familiar. Pope had also pedantically footnoted and prefaced his *The Dunciad Variorum* (1729), which had a Prolegomena by Scriblerus. Fielding had earlier used this pseudonym for his *Author's Farce*, and he would similarly add a Prolegomena to his *Covent-Garden Tragedy*.

After the summer of 1731, *The Tragedy of Tragedies*, and occasionally *Tom Thumb*, continued to be played, usually as an afterpiece. *The Tragedy of Tragedies* was presented with plays as various as *The Beggar's Opera* in 1769, *The Mourning Bride* in 1770, and *The Suspicious Husband* in 1775, with the comedian Kean as Glumdalca. The part of the princess Huncamunca, too, was sometimes taken by the comedian of the company. Drury Lane's farce comedian Harper played it in 1732.

H. W. Pedicord's search of the Drury Lane repertoire at the time of Garrick shows how continuously popular the play was.[9] *Tom Thumb* played for five seasons between 1747 and 1776, as opposed to three seasons for Wycherley's *The Country Wife* and one season for the Garrick version of Shakespeare's *Midsummer Night's Dream.* Even very popular plays like Shakespeare's *Merry Wives of Windsor* (thirteen seasons) and Congreve's *The Double Dealer* (seven seasons) were never performed more in a single season than *Tom Thumb* was. In 1755–56 *Tom Thumb* was performed five times. In their best seasons Congreve's play was performed three times and Shakespeare's three. This popularity is explained in part, but only in part, by the fact that *The Tragedy of Tragedies* was an afterpiece, and not a full evening's entertainment.

The play also had a life throughout the eighteenth century in North America. Hallam's English company performed it in New York City on 22 Oct. 1753. And the British Military Theatre (the officers of the garrison in New York City) put it on several times during the American Revolution. The first performance by them took place in January of 1777, shortly after Howe's capture of the city. After the Revolution the famous American actor Joseph Jefferson played Grizzle in 1798.[10] Although there is no adequate stage history for the nineteenth century, it is likely that the play continued as a stock piece into the nineteenth century. It is produced even today by amateur groups at American and British universities.

Perhaps the best testimony of the play's continued popularity is the adaptations. It was adapted as a ballad opera by Mrs Eliza Haywood and William Hatchett in 1733. The new version, called *The Opera of Operas*, added thirty-three airs to the text and set the whole burlesque in the popular rehearsal form, with appropriate comments by Sir Crit-Operatical. The airs were set to music twice in 1733, once by Thomas Arne for the Haymarket and once by J. F. Lampe for Drury Lane. Then in 1780 Kane O'Hara freely adapted it as *Tom Thumb, A Burletta.* Although no character name has become as pervasive as Swift's generic Yahoo, the names of some of the characters had so completely passed into common usage by the early part of the twentieth

[9] *The Theatrical Public in the Time of Garrick.* New York (King's Crown Press) 1954.

[10] See George C. D. Odell, *Annals of the New York Stage.* New York (Columbia U.P.) 1927.

century that Beatrix Potter used them for her mice in *The Tale of Two Bad Mice*.

When the play is produced today, and probably when it was produced later in the eighteenth century, most, if not all, of the political satire is lost to an audience unaware of the economic and diplomatic events of 1730. For that matter, most of the effect of the literary parody is now gone. An audience today can not even recognise parodies of lines from John Dryden or Edward Young, let alone from Elijah Fenton or John Banks. And the footnotes rather than delightfully confirming the literary parody, as they did for Fielding's audience, are only a literary curiosity for a twentieth-century reader. But something still remains. What remains is the sheer sense of farce bustle and activity, and Fielding's brilliant use of physical and verbal bathos. The bustle, the grand and pointless activity, and bathos continue to be satiric because they are aimed at something we have always with us, theatrical pretension.

A NOTE ON THE TEXTS

Tom Thumb

There were two quite distinct versions of *Tom Thumb* issued in 1730.[1] Both have precisely the same imprint: LONDON, | Printed: And Sold by J. ROBERTS in | *Warwick-Lane*. 1730. The title-pages and signatures differ, however. The title-page of the first issue is as follows: *TOM THUMB*. | A | TRAGEDY. | As it is Acted at the | THEATRE | IN THE | *HAY-MARKET*. | [rule] | [ornament] | [double rule]. This text is octavo printed on half sheets and the collation is: A^4, B-C^4, α^1. The title-page of the second version, of which there are three editions, is identical down to the first "rule" and then follows: Written by *Scriblerus Secundus*. | [rule] | — *Tragicus plerumque dolet Sermone pedestri*. Hor. | [rule]. This text is also octavo printed on half sheets. The collation is as follows: A-C^4, α^1.

Shortly after the first printing for opening night,[2] Fielding revised the play and released it under the pseudonym Scriblerus Secundus. The text of this issue is substantially the same as the text of the first issue. There are, however, six important insertions. A preface, prologue and epilogue are added; the bailiff scenes (II. I and II. II) are interpolated; and one additional speech is given to the King (II. VIII).

J. Roberts printed a second and a third edition of the revised play in 1730. The second edition is nothing more than a later impression of the first edition with the words "The SECOND EDITION" inserted into the title-page, between "rules", and after the Latin quotation. The words "The THIRD EDITION" are inserted in exactly the same place on the title-page of the third edition. The third edition, however, is clearly a separate edition. While the signatures remain the same, there is abundant evidence of resetting.

[1] *The Register of Books* records just one issue of *Tom Thumb. A Tragedy* in April of 1730.

[2] The first performance of *Tom Thumb* took place on 24 Apr. 1730 (see *The Daily Post* for that date); and on the page following the title-page of *Tom Thumb* there is an advertisement for *The Author's Farce*, published "this day . . . April 24, 1730".

J. T. Hillhouse, in his edition of the play, identifies and collates three editions. He uses what he calls the first edition as his copy text, inserting material from the "second" edition. However, he calls the first unsigned version his first edition, and he does not make it clear whether his second and third editions were recorded as second and third editions on the title-page. If they were, then he apparently did not collate the first edition of the revised play.

For this edition I have collated two copies of the first version (Folger Library and Bodleian Library) and two copies of the first edition of the second version (British Museum and Folger Library). I have also collated the second and third editions of the second version (British Museum). I have chosen the fuller first edition of the second version as my copy text because it represents Fielding's altered and final intention for *Tom Thumb*; I have noted all variations between this and the play as it was first issued. I have also accepted several corrections from the third edition, noting each in my Textual Notes.

Except for the following silent emendations, all variations from the copy text have been recorded in the Textual Notes. (*a*) The long "s" has been adjusted to modern usage and diphthongs have not been reproduced. (*b*) All abbreviations have been expanded. (*c*) Act and scene headings etc. have been regularised both typographically and with respect to punctuation. (*d*) Characters' names have always been given in caps and small caps throughout the paraphernalia; and the same form of their name is always given (*e.g.* the speech heading "Ld *Griz.*" is given as GRIZZLE). (*e*) The use of the single square bracke with stage directions in the copy text has been abolished. Square brackets are retained or introduced only to distinguish original stage directions from text matter where there is a possibility of confusion. Pointed brackets are used to enclose stage directions or additions to existing stage directions supplied by the editor. (*f*) Occasionally, the position of an *Aside* has been altered so that it appears in the text, before the speech to which it refers. (*g*) No attempt is made to reproduce display capitals, ornamental initials, factotums, or ornaments, or even to note their existence.

The Tragedy of Tragedies

Henry Fielding extensively revised his *Tom Thumb* for presentation on 24 Mar. 1731, perhaps justifying its being advertised as "Never Acted Before".[3] He even changed the name of the play, which like its predecessor was printed in time to be "sold at the theatre"[4] on opening night. It was now called THE | TRAGEDY | OF | *TRAGEDIES;* | OR THE | LIFE *and* DEATH | OF | TOM THUMB *the Great.* The imprint of this first edition of *The Tragedy of Tragedies* is— LONDON, | Printed; And Sold by *J. Roberts* in *Warwick-Lane.* | [rule] | M DCC XXXI. It was printed in octavo and signed A^4, $B\text{-}D^8$, E^4, F^2.

The text is stable through the several impressions of this edition as well as through later editions. In light of the general competence of eighteenth-century printers, this stability is not unusual. That is, it does not indicate that Roberts and later printers took more than usual care with this difficult text; it might only mean that Fielding made few, if any, additions or corrections to the proofs or to early impressions. Having rewritten the play, he seems simply to have turned it over to the printer.

J. T. Hillhouse, in his 1918 edition of the play, maintains that there is a single later impression of the first edition, which, he says "is identical with the first impression in title-page and in general form, but which contains a few corrections in spelling and punctuation."[5] I have been able to discover not one but four distinct "impressions", including the one recorded by Hillhouse.[6] Because there is no evidence of resetting, they are clearly multiple impressions of the same edition and not separate editions. Whether these are separate and distinct impressions with some lapse of time between each impression or merely texts which represent corrections in press is more difficult to assess.

Although it seems unlikely that an active printing house could afford

[3] *The London Stage, Part 3: 1729–1749*, ed. A. H. Scouten, p. 125. Carbondale, Ill. (Southern Ill. U.P.) 1961.

[4] *Ibid.* Also see *The Daily Post*, 23 Mar. 1731.

[5] Henry Fielding, *The Tragedy of Tragedies . . .*, ed. J. T. Hillhouse, p. 200.

[6] *The Register of Books* records just one edition of *The Tragedy of Tragedies* in March of 1731.

to have so much type bound up and lying idle even for a few days between impressions, this does seem to be the case. The corrections to the texts I have collated seem to indicate that these are separate and distinct impressions, and not corrections in press, because the corrections come in such neat and distinct stages and because I have found no corrected sheets from one stage bound in with uncorrected sheets from another stage.

In the texts I have examined, the corrections do seem to come in three stages. The first is to the title-page (outer forme A), the second to Act I, scenes I–V of text and footnotes (the outer and inner formes of B), and the third to the prefatory material (inner forme A) and to the text (outer forme of C). After these corrections to the early pages of the play, there seems to have been no attempt to adjust the minor corruptions of the text.

The copy of the play in the New York Public Library is the most corrupt text. That is, it is clearly the earliest impression. There are no corrections to any forme.

The copy in the possession of the Harvard Library and the three copies in the British Museum include only one correction to outer forme A. "Price One Shilling" is added after the imprint. Hillhouse apparently chose this impression, which I would call the second impression, for his copy text.

The copy in the University of Pennsylvania Library includes the corrections to both the outer and inner formes of B, as well as the correction to the title-page. All of these are the simplest proof reader's corrections: "undestand" becomes "understand" (I. i. 18 *e* 12); two unspaced words are corrected, "asa" becomes "as a" (I. III. 27 *z* 7); and one letter is added to a word to form the appropriate tense, "chose" becomes "choose" (I. III. 45). The Dublin edition of 1731 seems to be based on this impression. It does not contain the corruption introduced in the fourth impression, nor does it make at least one correction to page 15, inner forme B, that the fourth does.

I have not been able to locate Hillhouse's "second impression", what I would call the "fourth impression". It contains three additional corrections to the text: one to page iii (to inner forme A)—"concerninging" becomes "concerning" (line 1–2 of the Preface); one to page 15 (inner forme B)—a semi-colon is inserted after "We will" (I. V. 31); and one to page 21 (outer forme C)—an apostrophe is added to "Frays" to indicate elision. This text also includes one corruption: I. II. 23

reads "tho' *Rack*, in *Punch*, Eight Shillings be | Quart" rather than "be a | Quart". Apparently the slightly raised "a" at the end of the line, which had taken heavy ink in the earlier impressions, was lifted out in the inking process.

I have chosen the first impression (New York Public Library) as my copy text. This essentially differs from the text that Hillhouse used as his copy text only in imprint. I have judged this to be an earlier impression than the Harvard or British Museum texts for two reasons. First, its title-page is uncorrected. Second, there is some evidence of loosening type or at least ink build-up in the Harvard and British Museum copies. On several pages, shoulders of full-points and commas, at the end of lines, have printed, making them look like colons and semi-colons. In the N.Y.P. copy, this marking is barely discernible. I have incorporated any alterations from impressions later than the Harvard and British Museum copies that improve the reading of the text. Each alteration has been noted.

I have also collated the 1737 "third edition" (actually the second) of the play, the last edition but one put out in Fielding's lifetime and the last edition produced while he was an active dramatist. The printer J. Watts in Wild-Court near Lincolns-Inn Fields reprinted the play in 1737, perhaps because he felt that it had some clear political implications. This was the year of the Licensing Act and the year in which both *Pasquin* and *The Historical Register* were printed. *The Tragedy of Tragedies* was the only one of Fielding's early plays reprinted in that year or for several subsequent years.

For several reasons it is clear that the "third edition" was reprinted from printed copy rather than from manuscript. First, the printer was able to calculate the amount of text on each page so accurately that he was able to run the footnotes in double columns and save himself five pages. While this edition incorporates the corrections of the later impressions of the first edition, it also perpetuates a number of slight inaccuracies of that edition. For example, footnote *u* in II. VI cites "State of Innocency" rather than "State of Innocence", and footnote *n* in II. IX merely cites "Banks" rather than the more usual "Bank's Albion Queens" or "Albion Queens". Two lines later in footnote *n*, II. IX "Albion Queens" is cited when it should have been "Conquest of Granada". The compositor of the first edition had merely divided and transposed "Bank's Albion Queens", and the 1737 edition continues the error.

It is unlikely, in fact, that Fielding ever saw this new edition when it was being prepared. Fielding, according to G. E. Jensen,[7] was very careless about his texts even in their first printings. He often relegated proof reading to friends. "Fielding was not the sort of person to undertake the repunctuation and respelling of his text." Yet, the corrections in the 1737 text are almost entirely limited to just this kind of adjustment of accidentals. For instance, it consistently avoids separating subject from verb with a single comma. When it ventures into substantive corrections, it inevitably makes the sentence more correct and less colloquial, precisely the process that G. E. Jensen sees at work in the corrections to later editions of *Tom Jones*. He conjectures that there was a proof reader other than Fielding (perhaps Rev. William Young) because "idiom is often sacrificed for grammar" by this "pedantic busy-body".[8] So in *The Tragedy of Tragedies*, the "Author, I hope will be acknowledged by" (PREFACE 28–9) becomes the "Author, will be acknowledged, I hope, by" in the 1737 edition.

In a few instances where I have adjusted accidentals to improve comprehension, I have cited the "third edition" in my footnotes. I have done this not because I believe that the "third edition" has any real authority but merely to indicate that another eighteenth-century edition was so punctuated or arranged. For the same reason, I have, in several instances, cited the 1730 edition (*Tom Thumb*) when it is clear that Fielding was merely reproducing a scene as it had appeared in this earlier version of the play. The adjustments that I have made are in every case matters of compositorial chance, and I would have made them without the authority either of the earlier or the later edition simply to improve the reading of the text.

I have made the same silent alterations in this text that I have noted above in my note on the text for *Tom Thumb*. All other departures from the copy text have been reported in the Textual Notes.

[7] G. E. Jensen, "Proposals for a Definitive Edition of Fielding's *Tom Jones*", in *The Library*, XVIII (1937), p. 323.

[8] G. E. Jensen, *op. cit.*, p. 324.

PREFACE

A Preface is become almost as necessary to a Play, as a Prologue: It is a Word of Advice to the Reader, as the other to the Spectator: And as the Business of a Prologue is to commend the Play, so that of the Preface is to Compliment the Actors.

A Preface requires a Style entirely different from all other Writings; A Style for which I can find no Name in either the Sublime of *Longinus*, or the Profund of *Scriblerus*: which I shall therefore venture to call the Supernatural, after the celebrated Author of *Hurlothrumbo*: who, tho' no Writer of Prefaces, is a very great Master of their Style.

As *Charon* in *Lucian* suffers none to enter his Boat till stripped of every thing they have about them, so should no Word by any means enter into a Preface till stripped of all its Ideas. Mr. *Lock* complains of confused Ideas in Words, which is entirely amended by suffering them to give none at all: This may be done by adding, diminishing, or changing a Letter, as instead of *Paraphernalia*, writing *Paraphonalia*: For a Man may turn *Greek* into Nonsense, who cannot turn Sense into either *Greek* or *Latin*.

A Second Method of stripping Words of their Ideas is by putting half a dozen incoherent ones together: Such as *when the People of our Age shall be Ancestors*, &c. By which means one discordant Word, like a surly Man in Company, spoils the whole Sentence, and makes it entirely Prefatical.

Some imagine this Way of Writing to have been originally introduced by *Plato*, whom *Cicero* observes to have taken especial Pains in wrapping up his Sentiments from the Understandings of the Vulgar. But I can in no wise agree with them in this Conjecture, any more than their deriving the Word Preface, *quasi Plaface, a Plato*: whereas the Original Word is *Playface, quasi Players Face*: and sufficiently denotes some Player, who was as remarkable for his *Face*, as his Prefaces, to have been the Inventor of it.

But that the Preface to my Preface be not longer than that to my Play: I shall have done with the Performances of others, and speak a Word or two of my own.

This Preface then was writ at the Desire of my Bookseller, who told me that some Elegant Criticks had made three great Objections to this Tragedy: which I shall handle without any Regard to Precedence: And therefore I begin to defend the last Scene of my Play against the third Objection of these* *Kriticks*, which is, to the destroying all the Characters in it, this I cannot think so unprecedented as these Gentlemen would insinuate, having my-self known it done in the first Act of several Plays: Nay, it is common in modern Tragedy for the Characters to drop, like the Citizens in the first Scene of *OEdipus*, as soon as they come upon the Stage. 35 40

Secondly, they Object to the killing a Ghost. This (say they) far exceeds the Rules of Probability; perhaps it may; but I would desire these Gentlemen seriously to recollect, whether they have not seen in several celebrated Plays, such Expressions as these, *Kill my Soul*, *Stab my very Soul*, *Bleeding Soul*, *Dying Soul*, *cum multis aliis*, all which visibly confess that for a Soul or Ghost to be killed is no Impossibility. 45 50

As for the first Objection which they make, and the last which I answer, *viz*. to the Subject, to this I shall only say, that it is in the Choice of my Subject I have placed my chief Merit.

It is with great Concern that I have observed several of our (the *Grubstreet*) Tragical Writers, to Celebrate in their Immortal Lines the Actions of Heroes recorded in Historians and Poets, such as *Homer* or *Virgil*, *Livy* or *Plutarch*, the Propagation of whose Works is so apparently against the Interest of our Society; when the Romances, Novels, and Histories, *vulgo* call'd Story-Books, of our own People, furnish such abundant and proper Themes for their Pens, such are *Tom Tram*, *Hickathrift*, &c. 55 60

And here I congratulate my Cotemporary Writers, for their having enlarged the Sphere of Tragedy: The ancient Tragedy seems to have had only two Effects on an Audience, *viz*. It either awakened Terror and Compassion, or composed those and all other uneasy Sensations, by lulling the Audience in an agreeable Slumber. But to provoke the Mirth and Laughter of the Spectators, to join the Sock to the Buskin, is a Praise only due to Modern Tragedy. 65

Having spoken thus much of the Play, I shall proceed to the Performers, amongst whom if any shone brighter than the rest it was *Tom Thumb*. Indeed such was the Excellence thereof, that no 70

* *Prefatical Language.*

one can believe unless they see its Representation, to which I shall refer the Curious: Nor can I refrain from observing how well one of the Mutes set off his Part: So excellent was his Performance, that it out-did even my own Wishes: I gratefully give him my share of Praise, and desire the Audience to refer the whole to his beautiful Action.

And now I must return my hearty Thanks to the Musick, who, I believe, played to the best of their Skill, because it was for their own Reputation, and because they are paid for it: So have I thrown little *Tom Thumb* on the Town, and hope they will be favourable to him, and for an Answer to all Censures, take these Words of *Martial*,

Seria cum possim, quod delectantia malim
Scribere, Tu, Causa es —

PROLOGUE

By no Friend of the Author's.
Spoken by Mr. *JONES.*

With Mirth and Laughter to delight the Mind
The modern Tragedy was first design'd:
'Twas this made Farce *with* Tragedy *unite,*
And taught each Scribler in the Town to Write.

The Glorious Heroes who, in former Years, 5
Dissolv'd all Athens *and all* Rome *in Tears;*
Who to our Stage, have been transplanted too;
Whom Shakespear *taught to Storm, and* Lee *to Woo,*
And could to Softness, ev'ry Heart subdue,
Grub-Street *has turn'd to* Farce. — *Oh glorious Lane!* 10
O, may thy Authors never write in vain!
May crowded Theatres ne'er give Applause
To any other than the Grub-Street *Cause!*

Since then, to laugh, to Tragedies you come,
What Heroe is so proper as Tom Thumb? 15
Tom Thumb! *whose very Name must Mirth incite,*
And fill each merry Briton *with Delight.*

Britons, *awake!* — *Let* Greece *and* Rome *no more*
Their Heroes send to our Heroick Shore.
Let home-bred Subjects grace the modern Muse, 20
And Grub-Street *from her Self, her Heroes chuse:*
Her Story-Books *Immortalize in Fame,*
Hickathrift, Jack the Giant-Killer, *and* Tom Tram.
No Venus *shou'd in Sign-Post Painter shine;*
No Roman *Hero in a Scribler's Line:* 25
The monst'rous Dragon to the Sign belongs,
And Grub-Street's *Heroes best adorn her Songs.*
To-Night our Bard, Spectators, *would be* true
To Farce, *to* Tragedy, Tom Thumb, *and* You.
May all the Hissing Audience be struck Dumb; 30
Long live the Man who cries, Long live Tom Thumb.

EPILOGUE

Sent by an Unknown Hand.
Spoken by Miss *JONES.*

Tom Thumb, *twice Dead, is a third Time Reviv'd,*
And, by your Favour, may be yet long-liv'd.
But, more I fear the snarling Critick's Brow,
Than Grizzle's *Dagger, or the Throat of Cow!*
Well then — Toupees, I warrant you suppose 5
I'll be exceeding witty on the Beaus;
But faith! I come with quite a diff'rent View,
To shew there are Tom Thumbs, *as well as you.*
Place me upon the awful Bench, and try
If any Judge can sleep more sound than I. 10
Or let me o'er a Pulpit-Cushion peep,
See who can set you in a sounder Sleep.
Tom Thumb *can feel the Pulse, can give the Pill;*
No Doctor's Feather shall more surely kill.
I'll be a Courtier, give me but a Place*;* 15
A Title makes me equal with his Grace*:*
Lace but my Coat, where is a prettier Spark?
I'll be a Justice — give me but a Clerk.
A Poet too — when I have learnt to read,
And plunder both the Living and the Dead: 20
Any of these, Tom Thumb *with Ease can be,*
For Many such, are nothing more than He.

But, for the Ladies, they, I know, despise
The little Things of my inferior Size.
Their mighty Souls are all of them too large 25
To take so small a Heroe to their Charge.
Take Pity, Ladies, on a young Beginner;
Faith! I may prove, in time, a thumping Sinner.
Let your kind Smiles our Author's Cause defend;
He fears no Foes, while Beauty is his Friend. 30

DRAMATIS PERSONAE

MEN.

KING Arthur,	Mr. *Mullart.*
TOM THUMB,	Miss *Jones.*
Lord GRIZZLE,	Mr. *Jones.*
Mr. NOODLE,	Mr. *Reynolds.*
Mr. DOODLE,	Mr. *Marshall.*
1 PHYSICIAN,	Mr. *Hallam.*
2 PHYSICIAN,	Mr. *Dove.*

WOMEN.

QUEEN Dollalolla,	Mrs. *Mullart.*
Princess HUNCAMUNCA,	Mrs. *Jones.*
CLEORA,	Mrs. *Smith.*
MUSTACHA,	Mrs. *Clark.*

Courtiers, Slaves, Bailiffs, &c.

SCENE *The Court of King* Arthur.

ACT I

SCENE I

SCENE *The Palace.*
Mr. DOODLE, *Mr.* NOODLE.

DOODLE. Sure, such a Day as this was never seen!
The Sun himself, on this auspicious Day,
Shines like a Beau in a new Birth-Day Suit:
All Nature, O my *Noodle*! grins for Joy.
NOODLE. This Day, O Mr. *Doodle*! is a Day 5
Indeed, a Day we never saw before.
The mighty *Thomas Thumb* victorious comes;
Millions of Giants crowd his Chariot Wheels,
Who bite their Chains, and frown and foam like Mad-Dogs.
He rides, regardless of their ugly Looks. 10
So some Cock-Sparrow in a Farmer's Yard,
Hops at the Head of an huge Flock of Turkeys.
DOODLE. When Goody *Thumb* first brought this *Thomas* forth,
The *Genius* of our Land triumphant reign'd;
Then, then, O *Arthur*! did thy *Genius* reign. 15
NOODLE. They tell me, it is whisper'd in the Books
Of all our Sages, That this mighty Hero
(By *Merlin's* Art begot) has not a Bone
Within his Skin, but is a Lump of Gristle.
DOODLE. Wou'd *Arthur's* Subjects were such Gristle, all! 20
He then might break the Bones of ev'ry Foe.
NOODLE. But hark! these Trumpets speak the King's Approach.
DOODLE. He comes most luckily for my Petition!
Let us retire a little.

SCENE II

KING, QUEEN, *Lord* GRIZZLE, DOODLE, NOODLE.

KING. Let nothing but a Face of Joy appear;
The Man who frowns this Day, shall lose his Head,

Long may he live, as now, the Publick Joy,
While ev'ry Voice is burthen'd with his Praise.
TOM THUMB. Whisper, ye Winds! that *Huncamunca's* mine;
Ecchoes repeat, that *Huncamunca's* mine! 50
The dreadful Bus'ness of the War is over,
And Beauty, heav'nly Beauty! crowns the Toil.
I've thrown the bloody Garment now aside,
And *Hymeneal* Sweets invite my Bride.
So when some Chimney-Sweeper, all the Day, 55
Has through dark Paths pursu'd the Sooty Way,
At Night, to wash his Face and Hands he flies,
And in his t'other Shirt with his *Brickdusta* lies.

Exeunt all but GRIZZLE.

SCENE IV

Lord GRIZZLE, *Solus.*

GRIZZLE. See how the cringing Coxcombs fawn upon him!
The Sun-shine of a Court can, in a Day,
Ripen the vilest Insect to an Eagle:
And ev'ry little Wretch, who but an Hour
Before had scorn'd, and trod him under Feet, 5
Shall lift his Eyes aloft, to gaze at distance,
And flatter what they scorn'd.

SCENE V

Enter QUEEN, *to Lord* GRIZZLE.

QUEEN. Well met, my Lord.
You are the Man I sought. Have you not heard
(What ev'ry Corner of the Court resounds)
That little *Thumb* will be a great Man made.
GRIZZLE. I heard it, I confess — for who, alas! 5
Can always stop his Ears — but would my Teeth,
By grinding Knives, had first been set on Edge.
QUEEN. Would I had heard at the still Noon of Night,

Vain Impudence, if it be ever found
With Virtue, like the Trumpet in a Consort,
Drowns the sweet Musick of the softer Flute. 10
But say, my Boy, where didst thou leave the Giants?

TOM THUMB. My Liege, without the Castle Gates they stand,
The Castle Gates too low for their Admittance.

KING. What look they like?

TOM THUMB. Like twenty Things, my Liege; 15
Like twenty thousand Oaks, by Winter's Hand
Strip'd of their Blossoms; like a Range of Houses,
When Fire has burnt their Timber all away.

KING. Enough: The vast Idea fills my Soul;
I see them, yes, I see them now before me. 20
The monst'rous, ugly, barb'rous Sons of Whores,
Which, like as many rav'nous Wolves, of late
Frown'd grimly o'er the Land, like Lambs look now.
O *Thumb*, what do we to thy Valour owe!
The Princess *Huncamunca* is thy Prize. 25

QUEEN. Ha! Be still, my Soul!

TOM THUMB. Oh, happy, happy Hearing!
Witness, ye Stars! cou'd *Thumb* have ever set
A Bound to his Ambition — it had been
The Princess *Huncamunca*, in whose Arms 30
Eternity would seem but half an Hour.

QUEEN. Consider, Sir, reward your Soldier's Merit,
But give not *Huncamunca* to *Tom Thumb*.

KING. *Tom Thumb*! Odzooks, my wide extended Realm
Knows not a Name so glorious as *Tom Thumb*. 35
Not *Alexander*, in his highest Pride,
Could boast of Merits greater than *Tom Thumb*.
Not *Caesar*, *Scipio*, all the Flow'rs of *Rome*,
Deserv'd their Triumphs better than *Tom Thumb*.

QUEEN. Tho' greater yet his boasted Merit was, 40
He shall not have the Princess, that is Pos'.

KING. Say you so, Madam? We will have a Trial.
When I consent, what Pow'r has your Denyal?
For, when the Wife her Husband over-reaches,
Give him the Petticoat, and her the Breeches. 45

NOODLE. Long Health and Happiness attend the General!

Long may he live, as now, the Publick Joy,
While ev'ry Voice is burthen'd with his Praise.

TOM THUMB. Whisper, ye Winds! that *Huncamunca's* mine;
Ecchoes repeat, that *Huncamunca's* mine! 50
The dreadful Bus'ness of the War is over,
And Beauty, heav'nly Beauty! crowns the Toil.
I've thrown the bloody Garment now aside,
And *Hymeneal* Sweets invite my Bride.
So when some Chimney-Sweeper, all the Day, 55
Has through dark Paths pursu'd the Sooty Way,
At Night, to wash his Face and Hands he flies,
And in his t'other Shirt with his *Brickdusta* lies.

Exeunt all but GRIZZLE.

SCENE IV

Lord GRIZZLE, *Solus.*

GRIZZLE. See how the cringing Coxcombs fawn upon him!
The Sun-shine of a Court can, in a Day,
Ripen the vilest Insect to an Eagle:
And ev'ry little Wretch, who but an Hour
Before had scorn'd, and trod him under Feet, 5
Shall lift his Eyes aloft, to gaze at distance,
And flatter what they scorn'd.

SCENE V

Enter QUEEN, *to Lord* GRIZZLE.

QUEEN. Well met, my Lord.
You are the Man I sought. Have you not heard
(What ev'ry Corner of the Court resounds)
That little *Thumb* will be a great Man made.

GRIZZLE. I heard it, I confess — for who, alas! 5
Can always stop his Ears — but would my Teeth,
By grinding Knives, had first been set on Edge.

QUEEN. Would I had heard at the still Noon of Night,

ACT I

SCENE I

SCENE *The Palace.*
Mr. DOODLE, *Mr.* NOODLE.

DOODLE. Sure, such a Day as this was never seen!
The Sun himself, on this auspicious Day,
Shines like a Beau in a new Birth-Day Suit:
All Nature, O my *Noodle*! grins for Joy.
NOODLE. This Day, O Mr. *Doodle*! is a Day 5
Indeed, a Day we never saw before.
The mighty *Thomas Thumb* victorious comes;
Millions of Giants crowd his Chariot Wheels,
Who bite their Chains, and frown and foam like Mad-Dogs.
He rides, regardless of their ugly Looks. 10
So some Cock-Sparrow in a Farmer's Yard,
Hops at the Head of an huge Flock of Turkeys.
DOODLE. When Goody *Thumb* first brought this *Thomas* forth,
The *Genius* of our Land triumphant reign'd;
Then, then, O *Arthur*! did thy *Genius* reign. 15
NOODLE. They tell me, it is whisper'd in the Books
Of all our Sages, That this mighty Hero
(By *Merlin's* Art begot) has not a Bone
Within his Skin, but is a Lump of Gristle.
DOODLE. Wou'd *Arthur's* Subjects were such Gristle, all! 20
He then might break the Bones of ev'ry Foe.
NOODLE. But hark! these Trumpets speak the King's Approach.
DOODLE. He comes most luckily for my Petition!
Let us retire a little.

SCENE II

KING, QUEEN, *Lord* GRIZZLE, DOODLE, NOODLE.

KING. Let nothing but a Face of Joy appear;
The Man who frowns this Day, shall lose his Head,

That he may have no Face to frown again.
Smile, *Dollalolla*; — Ha! what wrinkled Sorrow
Sits, like some *Mother Demdike*, on thy Brow? 5
Whence flow those Tears fast down thy blubber'd Cheeks,
Like a swoln Gutter, gushing through the Streets?

QUEEN. Excess of Joy, my Lord, I've heard Folks say,
Gives Tears, as often as Excess of Grief.

KING. If it be so, let all Men cry for Joy, 10
'Till my whole Court be drowned with their Tears;
Nay, 'till they overflow my utmost Land,
And leave me nothing but the Sea to rule.

DOODLE. My Liege! I've a Petition —

KING. Petition me no Petitions, Sir, to-day; 15
Let other Hours be set apart for Bus'ness.
To-day it is our Pleasure to be drunk,
And this our Queen shall be as drunk as Us.

QUEEN. If the capacious Goblet overflow
With *Arrack-Punch* — 'fore *George*! I'll see it out; 20
Of *Rum*, or *Brandy*, I'll not taste a Drop.

KING. Tho' *Rack*, in *Punch*, Eight Shillings be a Quart,
And *Rum* and *Brandy* be no more than Six,
Rather than quarrel, you shall have your Will.

Trumpets.

But, ha! the Warrior comes; *Tom Thumb* approaches; 25
The welcome Hero, Giant-killing Lad,
Preserver of my Kingdom, is arrived.

SCENE III

TOM THUMB, *attended*; KING, QUEEN, *Lord* GRIZZLE, DOODLE, NOODLE.

KING. O welcome, ever welcome to my Arms,
My dear *Tom Thumb*! How shall I thank thy Merit?

TOM THUMB. By not b'ing thank'd at all, I'm thank'd enough;
My Duty I have done, and done no more.

QUEEN. [*Aside.*] Was ever such a lovely Creature seen! 5

KING. Thy Modesty's a Candle to thy Merit,
It shines Itself, and shews thy Merit too.

The dreadful Cry of Fire in ev'ry Street!
Odsbobs! I could almost destroy my self, 10
To think I should a Grand-mother be made
By such a Rascal. — Sure, the King forgets,
When in a Pudding, by his Mother put,
The Bastard, by a Tinker, on a Stile
Was drop'd. — O, good Lord *Grizzle*! can I bear 15
To see him, from a Pudding, mount the Throne?

GRIZZLE. Oh Horror! Horror! Horror! cease my Queen,
Thy Voice, like twenty Screech-Owls, wracks my Brain.

QUEEN. Then rouze thy Spirit — we may yet prevent
This hated March. — 20

GRIZZLE. We will. — Not Fate, itself,
Should it conspire with *Thomas Thumb*, should cause it.
I'll swim through Seas; I'll ride upon the Clouds;
I'll dig the Earth; I'll blow out ev'ry Fire;
I'll rave; I'll rant; I'll rush; I'll rise; I'll roar 25
Fierce as the Man whom smiling Dolphins bore,
From the Prosaick to Poetick Shore.
I'll tear the Scoundrel into twenty Pieces.

QUEEN. Oh, no! prevent the Match, but hurt him not;
For, tho' I would not have him have my Daughter, 30
Yet, can we kill the Man who kill'd the Giants?

GRIZZLE. I tell you, Madam, it was all a Trick,
He made the Giants first, and then he kill'd them;
As Fox-hunters bring Foxes to a Wood,
And then with Hounds they drive them out again. 35

QUEEN. How! Have you seen no Giants? Are there not
Now, in the Yard, ten thousand proper Giants?

GRIZZLE. Indeed, I cannot positively tell,
But firmly do believe there is not One.

QUEEN. Hence! from my Sight! thou Traytor, hie away; 40
By all my Stars! thou enviest *Tom Thumb*.
Go, Sirrah! go; hie away! hie! — thou art
A Setting-Dog — and like one I use thee.

GRIZZLE. Madam, I go.
Tom Thumb shall feel the Vengeance you have rais'd. 45
So when two Dogs are fighting in the Streets,
With a third Dog, one of the two Dogs meets,

With angry Teeth, he bites him to the Bone,
And this Dog smarts for what that Dog had done. *Exit.*

SCENE VI

QUEEN, *Sola.*

QUEEN. And whither shall I go? — Alack-a-day!
I love *Tom Thumb* — but must not tell him so;
For what's a Woman, when her Virtue's gone?
A Coat without its Lace; Wig out of Buckle;
A Stocking with a Hole in't. — I can't live 5
Without my Virtue, or without *Tom Thumb.*
Then let me weigh them in two equal Scales,
In this Scale put my Virtue, that, *Tom Thumb.*
Alas! *Tom Thumb* is heavier than my Virtue.
But hold! — Perhaps I may be left a Widow: 10
This Match prevented, then *Tom Thumb* is mine,
In that dear Hope, I will forget my Pain.
So when some Wench to *Tothill-Bridewell's* sent,
With beating Hemp, and Flogging, she's content;
She hopes, in Time, to ease her present Pain; 15
At length is free, and walks the Streets again. *Exit.*

ACT II

SCENE I

SCENE *The Street.*
BAILIFF, FOLLOWER.

BAILIFF. Come on, my trusty Follower, inur'd
To ev'ry kind of Danger; cudgell'd oft;
Often in Blankets toss'd — oft Pump'd upon:
Whose Virtue in a Horse-Pond hath been try'd.
Stand here by me. — This way must *Noodle* pass. 5
FOLLOWER. Were he an Half-pay Officer, a Bully,
A Highway-man, or Prize-fighter, I'd nab him.
BAILIFF. This Day discharge thy Duty, and at Night
A double Mug of Beer and Beer shall glad thee.

Then in an Ale-house may'st thou sit at Ease, 10
And quite forget the Labours of the Day.
So wearied Oxen to their Stalls retire,
And rest from all the Burthens of the Plough.

FOLLOWER. No more, no more, O Bailiff! ev'ry Word
Inspires my Soul with Virtue. — O! I long 15
To meet the Enemy in the Street — and nab him;
To lay arresting Hands upon his Back,
And drag him trembling to the Spunging-House.

BAILIFF. There, when I have him, I will spunge upon him.
O glorious Thought! By the Sun, Moon, and Stars, 20
I will enjoy it, tho' it be in Thought!
Yes, yes, my Follower, I will enjoy it.
So Lovers, in Imagination strong,
Enjoy their absent Mistresses in Thought,
And hug their Pillows, as I now do thee: 25
And as they squeeze its Feathers out — so I
Would from his Pockets squeeze the Money out.

FOLLOWER. Alas! too just your Simile, I fear,
For Courtiers often nothing are but Feathers.

BAILIFF. Oh, my good Follower! when I reflect 30
On the big Hopes I once had entertain'd,
To see the Law, as some devouring Wolf,
Eat up the Land, — 'till, like a Garrison,
Its whole Provision's gone, — Lawyers were forc'd,
For want of Food, to feed on one another. 35
But Oh! fall'n Hope. The Law will be reduc'd
Again to Reason, whence it first arose.
But Ha! our Prey approaches — let us retire.

SCENE II

TOM THUMB, NOODLE, BAILIFF, FOLLOWER.

TOM THUMB. Trust me, my *Noodle*, I am wond'rous sick;
For tho' I love the gentle *Huncamunca*,
Yet at the Thought of Marriage, I grow pale;
For Oh! — but swear thou'lt keep it ever secret,
I will unfold a Tale will make thee stare. 5

NOODLE. I swear by lovely *Huncamunca's* Charms.
TOM THUMB. Then know — My Grand-mamma hath often said —
Tom Thumb, beware of Marriage. —
NOODLE. Sir, I blush
To think a Warrior great in Arms as you, 10
Should be affrighted by his Grand-mamma.
Can an old Woman's empty Dreams deter
The blooming Hero from the Virgin's Arms?
Think of the Joy which will your Soul alarm,
When in her fond Embraces clasp'd you lie, 15
While on her panting Breast dissolv'd in Bliss,
You pour out all *Tom Thumb* in ev'ry Kiss.
TOM THUMB. Oh, *Noodle*! thou hast fir'd my eager Soul;
Spight of my Grandmother, she shall be mine;
I'll hug, caress, I'll eat her up with Love. 20
Whole Days, and Nights, and Years shall be too short
For our Enjoyment; ev'ry Sun shall rise
Blushing, to see us in our Bed together.
NOODLE. Oh, Sir! this Purpose of your Soul pursue.
BAILIFF. Oh, Sir! I have an Action against you. 25
NOODLE. At whose Suit is it?
BAILIFF. At your Taylor's, Sir.
Your Taylor put this Warrant in my Hands,
And I arrest you, Sir, at his Commands.
TOM THUMB. Ha! Dogs! Arrest my Friend before my Face! 30
Think you *Tom Thumb* will swallow this Disgrace!
But let vain Cowards threaten by their Word,
Tom Thumb shall show his Anger by his Sword.

Kills the BAILIFF.

BAILIFF. Oh, I am slain!
FOLLOWER. I'm murdered also, 35
And to the Shades, the dismal Shades below,
My Bailiff's faithful Follower I go.
TOM THUMB. Thus perish all the Bailiffs in the Land,
'Till Debtors at Noon-day shall walk the Street,
And no one fear a Bailiff, or his Writ. 40

SCENE III

The Princess HUNCAMUNCA's *Apartment.*
HUNCAMUNCA, CLEORA, MUSTACHA.

HUNCAMUNCA. Give me some Musick to appease my Soul:
Gentle *Cleora*, sing my fav'rite Song.

CLEORA *sings.*
Cupid, *ease a Love-sick Maid,*
Bring thy Quiver to her Aid;
With equal Ardor wound the Swain: 5
Beauty should never sigh in vain.
Let him feel the pleasing Smart,
Drive thy Arrow through his Heart;
When One you wound, you then destroy;
When Both you kill, you kill with Joy. 10

HUNCAMUNCA. O, *Tom Thumb! Tom Thumb!* wherefore art thou *Tom Thumb?*
Why had'st thou not been born of Royal Blood?
Why had not mighty *Bantam* been thy Father?
Or else the King of *Brentford*, *Old* or *New*?

MUSTACHA. I am surprized that your Highness can give your 15 self a Moment's Uneasiness about that little insignificant Fellow, *Tom Thumb*. One properer for a Play-thing than a Husband.— Were he my Husband, his Horns should be as long as his Body.— If you had fallen in Love with a Grenadier, I should not have wondered at it. If you had fallen in Love with Something; but to 20 fall in Love with Nothing!

HUNCAMUNCA. Ceace, my *Mustacha*, on your Duty cease.
The *Zephyr*, when in flowry Vales it plays,
Is not so soft, so sweet as *Thummy*'s Breath.
The Dove is not so gentle to its Mate. 25

MUSTACHA. The Dove is every bit as proper for a Husband. Alas! Madam, there's not a Beau about the Court that looks so little like a Man. He is a perfect Butterfly, a Thing without Substance, and almost without Shadow too.

HUNCAMUNCA. This Rudeness is unseasonable; desist, 30
Or I shall think this Railing comes from Love.

Tom Thumb's a Creature of that charming Form,
That no one can abuse, unless they love him.
CLEORA. Madam, the King.

SCENE IV

KING, HUNCAMUNCA.

KING. Let all but *Huncamunca* leave the Room.

Exit CLEORA, *and* MUSTACHA.

Daughter, I have of late observ'd some Grief
Unusual in your Countenance, your Eyes
That, like two open Windows, us'd to shew
The lovely Beauty of the Room within, 5
Have now two Blinds before them — What is the Cause?
Say, have you not enough of Meat or Drink?
We've giv'n strict Orders not to have you stinted.
HUNCAMUNCA. Alas! my Lord, a tender Maid may want
What she can neither Eat nor Drink — 10
KING. What's that?
HUNCAMUNCA. Oh! Spare my Blushes, but I mean a Husband.
KING. If that be all, I have provided one,
A Husband great in Arms, whose Warlike Sword
Streams with the yellow Blood of slaughter'd Giants. 15
Whose Name in *Terrâ incognitâ* is known,
Whose Valour, Wisdom, Virtue make a Noise,
Great as the Kettle Drums of twenty Armies.
HUNCAMUNCA. Whom does my Royal Father mean?
KING. *Tom Thumb.* 20
HUNCAMUNCA. Is it possible?
KING. Ha! the Window-Blinds are gone,
A Country Dance of Joys is in your Face,
Your Eyes spit Fire, your Cheeks grow red as Beef.
HUNCAMUNCA. O, there's a Magick-musick in that Sound, 25
Enough to turn me into Beef indeed.
Yes, I will own, since licens'd by your Word,
I'll own *Tom Thumb* the Cause of all my Grief.
For him I've Sigh'd, I've Wept, I've gnaw'd my Sheets.

SCENE V

KING, HUNCAMUNCA, DOODLE.

DOODLE. Oh! fatal News — the great *Tom Thumb* is dead.
KING. How dead!
DOODLE. Alas! as dead as a Door-Nail.
Help, help, the Princess faints!
KING. Fetch her a Dram. 5
HUNCAMUNCA. Under my Bed you'll find a Quart of Rum.

Exit DOODLE.

KING. Dow does my pretty Daughter?
HUNCAMUNCA. Thank you, Papa,
I'm something better now.

Enter SLAVE.

KING. What Slave waits there? 10
Go order the Physicians strait before me,
That did attend *Tom Thumb* — now by my Stars,
Unless they give a full and true Account
Of his Distemper, they shall all be hang'd.
DOODLE. [*returns.*] Here is the Bottle, and here is the Glass. 15
I found them both together —
KING. Give them me.

fills the Glass.

Drink it all off, it will do you no harm.

SCENE VI

KING, HUNCAMUNCA, DOODLE, PHYSICIANS.

1 PHYSICIAN. We here attend your Majesty's Command.
KING. Of what Distemper did *Tom Thumb* demise?
1 PHYSICIAN. He died, may it please your Majesty, of a Distemper which *Paracelsus* calls the *Diaphormane*, *Hippocrates* the *Catecumen*, *Galen* the *Regon*—He was taken with a Dizziness in 5
his Head, for which I bled him, and put on Four Blisters—he

then had the Gripes, wherefore I thought it proper to apply a Glister, a Purge, and a Vomit.

2 PHYSICIAN. Doctor, you mistake the Case; the Distemper was not the *Diaphormane*, as you vainly imagine; it was the *Peripilusis* — and tho' I approve very much of all that you did — let me tell you, you did not do half enough — you know he complained of a Pain in his Arm, I would immediately have cut off his Arm, and have laid open his Head, to which I would have applied some *Trahifick* Plaister; after that I would have proceeded to my *Cathartricks*, *Emeticks*, and *Diureticks*. 10 15

1 PHYSICIAN. In the *Peripilusis* indeed these Methods are not only wholesome but necessary: but in the *Diaphormane* otherwise.

2 PHYSICIAN. What are the Symptoms of the *Diaphormane*? 20

1 PHYSICIAN. They are various—very various and uncertain.

2 PHYSICIAN. Will you tell me that a Man died of the *Diaphormane* in one Hour—when the Crisis of that Distemper does not rise till the Fourth Day?

1 PHYSICIAN. The Symptoms are various, very various and uncertain. 25

SCENE VII

To them. TOM THUMB *attended.*

TOM THUMB. Where is the Princess? where's my *Huncamunca*?
Lives she? O happy *Thumb*! for even now
A Murmur humming skips about the Court,
That *Huncamunca* was defunct.

KING. Bless me! 5
Ye Blazing Stars — sure 'tis Illusion all.
Are you *Tom Thumb*, and are you too alive?

TOM THUMB. *Tom Thumb* I am, and eke also alive.

KING. And have you not been dead at all? —

TOM THUMB. Not I. 10

1 PHYSICIAN. I told you, Doctor, that *Cathartick* would do his Business.

2 PHYSICIAN. Ay, and I am very much surprized to find it did not.

SCENE VIII

KING, TOM THUMB, HUNCAMUNCA, PHYSICIANS, DOODLE, NOODLE.

NOODLE. Great News, may it please your Majesty, I bring,
A Traytor is discover'd, who design'd
To kill *Tom Thumb* with Poison.
KING. Ha! say you?
NOODLE. A Girl had dress'd her Monkey in his Habit, 5
And that was poisoned by mistake for *Thumb*.
KING. Here are Physicians for you, whose nice Art
Can take a dress'd up Monkey for a Man.
Come to my Arms, my dearest Son-in-Law!
Happy's the wooing, that's not long a doing; 10
Proceed we to the Temple, there to tye
The burning Bridegroom to the blushing Bride.
And if I guess aright, *Tom Thumb* this Night
Shall give a Being to a new *Tom Thumb*.
TOM THUMB. It shall be my Endeavour so to do. 15
HUNCAMUNCA. O fie upon you, Sir, you make me blush.
TOM THUMB. It is the Virgin's sign, and suits you well —
I know not where, nor how, nor what I am,
I'm so transported, I have lost my self.
HUNCAMUNCA. Forbid it, all the Stars; for you're so small, 20
That were you lost, you'd find your self no more.
So the unhappy Sempstress, once, they say,
Her Needle in a Pottle, lost, of Hay.
In vain she look'd, and look'd, and made her Moan;
For ah! the Needle was for ever gone. 25
KING. Long may ye live, and love, and propagate,
'Till the whole Land be peopled with *Tom Thumbs*.
So when the *Cheshire*-Cheese a Maggot breeds,
Another and another still succeeds;
By thousands and ten thousands they encrease, 30
Till one continu'd Maggot fills the rotten Cheese.

SCENE IX

Manent PHYSICIANS.

1 PHYSICIAN. Pray, Doctor *Church-yard*, what is your *Peripilusis*? I did not care to own my Ignorance to the King; but I never heard of such a Distemper before.

2 PHYSICIAN. Truly, Doctor *Fillgrave*, it is more nearly allied to the *Diaphormane* than you imagine—and when you know the one, you will not be very far from finding out the other. But it is now past Ten; I must haste to Lord *Weekleys*, for he'll be dead before Eleven, and so I shall lose my Fee. 5

1 PHYSICIAN. Doctor, your Servant.

Exeunt severally.

SCENE X

Enter QUEEN *sola.*

QUEEN. How am I forc'd to wander thus alone,
As if I were the *Phaenix* of my Kind;
Tom Thumb is lost — yet *Hickathrift* remains,
And *Hickathrift's* as great a Man as *Thumb.*
Be he then our Gallant — but ha! what Noise 5
Comes trav'ling onward, bellowing as loud
As Thunder rumbling through th' AEtherial Plains?

SCENE XI

KING, QUEEN, HUNCAMUNCA, *Courtiers.*

KING. Open the Prisons, set the Wretched free,
And bid our Treasurer disburse Six Pounds
To pay their Debts. — Let no one weep to-day.
Come, my fair Consort, sit thee down by me.
Here seated, let us view the Dancers Sport; 5
Bid them advance. — This is the Wedding-Day
Of Princess *Huncamunca* and *Tom Thumb.*

Dance, *Epithalamium, and* Sports.

SCENE *The Last*

NOODLE, KING, QUEEN, HUNCAMUNCA, *Courtiers.*

NOODLE. Oh monstrous! dreadful! terrible! Oh! Oh!
Deaf be my Ears, for ever blind my Eyes,
Dumb be my Tongue, Feet lame, all Senses lost.
KING. What does the Blockhead mean?
NOODLE. Whilst from my Garret 5
I look'd abroad into the Street below,
I saw *Tom Thumb* attended by the Mob,
Twice Twenty Shoe-boys, twice two Dozen Links,
Chairmen, and Porters, Hackney-Coachmen, Whores;
When on the sudden through the Streets there came 10
A Cow, of larger than the usual Size,
And in a Moment, guess, oh! guess the rest,
And in a Moment swallow'd up *Tom Thumb.*
KING. Horrible indeed!
GRIZZLE. Swallowed she him alive? 15
NOODLE. Alive, alive, Lord *Grizzle*; so the Boys
Of Fishmongers do swallow Gudgeons down.
GRIZZLE. [*Aside.*] Curse on the Cow that took my Vengeance from me.
KING. Shut up again the Prisons, bid my Treasurer
Not give three Farthings out — hang all the *Culprits*, 20
Guilty or not — no matter. — Ravish Virgins,
Go bid the School-masters whip all their Boys;
Let Lawyers, Parsons, and Physicians loose,
To rob, impose on, and to kill the World.

Ghost of TOM THUMB *rises.*

GHOST. *Tom Thumb* I am — but am not eke alive. 25
My Body's in the Cow, my Ghost is here.
GRIZZLE. Thanks, O ye Stars, my Vengenace is restor'd,
Nor shalt thou fly me — for I'll kill thy Ghost.
Kills the Ghost.

HUNCAMUNCA. O barbarous Deed! — I will revenge him so.
Kills GRIZZLE.

DOODLE. Ha! *Grizzle* kill'd — then Murtheress beware. 30

Kills HUNCAMUNCA.

QUEEN. O Wretch! — have at thee.

Kills DOODLE.

NOODLE. And have at thee too.

Kills the QUEEN.

CLEORA. Thou'st kill'd the Queen.

Kills NOODLE.

MUSTACHA. And thou hast kill'd my Lover.

Kills CLEORA.

KING. Ha! Murtheress vile, take that.

Kills MUSTACHA. 35

And take thou this.

Kills himself, and falls.

So when the Child whom Nurse from Mischief guards,
Sends *Jack* for Mustard with a Pack of Cards;
Kings, Queens and Knaves, throw one another down,
'Till the whole Pack lies scatter'd and o'erthrown; 40
So all our Pack upon the Floor is cast,
And all I boast is, that I fall the last.

Dies.

FINIS.

THE TRAGEDY OF TRAGEDIES

great Praise of our Author, that, however imperfect the former was, still did even that faint Resemblance of the true *Tom Thumb*, contain sufficient Beauties to give it a Run of upwards of Forty Nights, to the politest Audiences. But, nothwithstanding that Applause which it receiv'd from all the best Judges, it was as severely censured by some few bad ones, and I believe, rather maliciously than ignorantly, reported to have been intended a Burlesque on the loftiest Parts of Tragedy, and designed to banish what we generally call Fine Things, from the Stage. 35

Now, if I can set my Country right in an Affair of this Importance, I shall lightly esteem any Labour which it may cost. And this I the rather undertake, First, as it is indeed in some measure incumbent on me to vindicate myself from that surreptitious Copy beforementioned, published by some ill-meaning People, under my Name: Secondly, as knowing my self more capable of doing Justice to our Author, than any other Man, as I have given my self more Pains to arrive at a thorough Understanding of this little Piece, having for ten Years together read nothing else; in which time, I think I may modestly presume, with the help of my English Dictionary, to comprehend all the Meanings of every Word in it. 40 45 50

But should any Error of my Pen awaken *Clariss. Bentleium* to enlighten the World with his Annotations on our Author, I shall not think that the least Reward or Happiness arising to me from these my Endeavours.

I shall wave at present, what hath caused such Feuds in the learned World, Whether this Piece was originally written by *Shakespear*, tho' certainly That, were it true, must add a considerable Share to its Merit; especially, with such who are so generous as to buy and to commend what they never read, from an implicit Faith in the Author only: A Faith! which our Age abounds in as much, as it can be called deficient in any other. 55 60

Let it suffice, that the *Tragedy of Tragedies*, or, *The Life and Death of Tom Thumb*, was written in the Reign of Queen *Elizabeth*. Nor can the Objection made by Mr. *D*——, That the Tragedy must then have been antecedent to the History, have any Weight, when we consider, That tho' the *History of Tom Thumb*, printed by and for *Edward M*——*r*, at the Looking-Glass on *London-Bridge*, be of a later Date; still must we suppose this History to have been transcribed from some other, unless we suppose the Writer there- 65

H. Scriblerus Secundus;

HIS

PREFACE

The Town hath seldom been more divided in its Opinion, than concerning the Merit of the following Scenes. Whilst some publickly affirmed, That no Author could produce so fine a Piece but Mr. *P*——, others have with as much Vehemence insisted, That no one could write any thing so bad, but Mr. *F*——.

Nor can we wonder at this Dissention about its Merit, when the learned World have not unanimously decided even the very Nature of this Tragedy. For tho' most of the Universities in *Europe* have honoured it with the Name of *Egregium & maximi pretii opus, Tragaediis tam antiquis quam novis longe anteponendum;* nay, Dr. *B*—— hath pronounced, *Citiùs Maevii AEneadem quam Scribleri istius Tragaediam hanc crediderim, cujus Autorem Senecam ipsum tradidisse haud dubitârim*; and the great Professor *Burman*, hath stiled *Tom Thumb, Heroum omnium Tragicorum facilè Principem.* Nay, tho' it hath, among other Languages, been translated into *Dutch*, and celebrated with great Applause at *Amsterdam* (where Burlesque never came) by the Title of *Mynheer Vander Thumb*, the Burgomasters receiving it with that reverent and silent Attention, which becometh an Audience at a deep Tragedy: Notwithstanding all this, there have not been wanting some who have represented these Scenes in a ludicrous Light; and Mr. *D*—— hath been heard to say, with some Concern, That he wondered a Tragical and Christian Nation would permit a Representation on its Theatre, so visibly designed to ridicule and extirpate every thing that is Great and Solemn among us.

This learned Critick, and his Followers, were led into so great an Error, by that surreptitious and piratical Copy which stole last Year into the World; with what Injustice and Prejudice to our Author, I hope will be acknowledged by every one who shall happily peruse this genuine and original Copy. Nor can I help remarking, to the great Praise of our Author, that, however imperfect the former was, still did even that faint Resemblance of the true *Tom Thumb*, contain sufficient Beauties to give it a Run of upwards of Forty Nights, to the politest Audiences. But, nothwithstanding that Applause which it receiv'd from all the best Judges, it was as severely censured by some few bad ones, and I believe, rather maliciously than ignorantly, reported to have been intended a Burlesque on the loftiest Parts of Tragedy, and designed to banish what we generally call Fine Things, from the Stage. 35

Now, if I can set my Country right in an Affair of this Importance, I shall lightly esteem any Labour which it may cost. And this I the rather undertake, First, as it is indeed in some measure incumbent on me to vindicate myself from that surreptitious Copy beforementioned, published by some ill-meaning People, under my Name: Secondly, as knowing my self more capable of doing Justice to our Author, than any other Man, as I have given my self more Pains to arrive at a thorough Understanding of this little Piece, having for ten Years together read nothing else; in which time, I think I may modestly presume, with the help of my English Dictionary, to comprehend all the Meanings of every Word in it. 40 45 50

But should any Error of my Pen awaken *Clariss. Bentleium* to enlighten the World with his Annotations on our Author, I shall not think that the least Reward or Happiness arising to me from these my Endeavours.

I shall wave at present, what hath caused such Feuds in the learned World, Whether this Piece was originally written by *Shakespear*, tho' certainly That, were it true, must add a considerable Share to its Merit; especially, with such who are so generous as to buy and to commend what they never read, from an implicit Faith in the Author only: A Faith! which our Age abounds in as much, as it can be called deficient in any other. 55 60

Let it suffice, that the *Tragedy of Tragedies*, or, *The Life and Death of Tom Thumb*, was written in the Reign of Queen *Elizabeth*. Nor can the Objection made by Mr. *D*——, That the Tragedy must then have been antecedent to the History, have any Weight, when we consider, That tho' the *History of Tom Thumb*, printed by and for *Edward M*——*r*, at the Looking-Glass on *London-Bridge*, be of a later Date; still must we suppose this History to have been transcribed from some other, unless we suppose the Writer there- 65

THE TRAGEDY OF TRAGEDIES

of to be inspired: A Gift very faintly contended for by the Writers 70
of our Age. As to this History's not bearing the Stamp of Second,
Third, or Fourth Edition, I see but little in that Objection; Editions
being very uncertain Lights to judge of Books by: And perhaps
Mr. *M——r* may have joined twenty Editions in one, as Mr.
C——l hath ere now divided one into twenty. 75

Nor doth the other Argument, drawn from the little Care our
Author hath taken to keep up to the Letter of the History, carry any
greater Force. Are there not Instances of Plays, wherein the History
is so perverted, that we can know the Heroes whom they
celebrate by no other Marks than their Names? Nay, do we not find 80
the same Character placed by different Poets in such different Lights,
that we can discover not the least Sameness, or even Likeness in the
Features? The *Sophonisba* of *Mairet*, and of *Lee*, is a tender, passionate,
amorous Mistress of *Massinissa*; *Corneille*, and Mr. *Thomson*
give her no other Passion but the Love of her Country, and make 85
her as cool in her Affection to *Massinissa*, as to *Syphax*. In the two
latter, she resembles the Character of Queen *Elizabeth*; in the two
former she is the Picture of *Mary* Queen of *Scotland*. In short, the
one *Sophonisba* is as different from the other, as the *Brutus* of *Voltaire*,
is from the *Marius* Jun. of *Otway*; or as the *Minerva* is from 90
the *Venus* of the Ancients.

Let us now proceed to a regular Examination of the Tragedy
before us, in which I shall treat separately of the Fable, the Moral,
the Characters, the Sentiments, and the Diction. And first of the

Fable; which I take to be the most simple imaginable; and, to use 95
the Words of an eminent Author, 'One, regular, and uniform, not
'charged with a Multiplicity of Incidents, and yet affording several
'Revolutions of Fortune; by which the Passions may be excited,
'varied, and driven to their full Tumult of Emotion.' — Nor is the
Action of this Tragedy less great than uniform. The Spring of all, 100
is the Love of *Tom Thumb* for *Huncamunca*; which causeth the
Quarrel between their Majesties in the first Act; the Passion of Lord
Grizzle in the Second; the Rebellion, Fall of Lord *Grizzle*, and
Glumdalca, Devouring of *Tom Thumb* by the Cow, and that bloody
Catastrophe, in the Third. 105

Nor is the *Moral* of this excellent Tragedy less noble than the
Fable; it teaches these two instructive Lessons, *viz*. That Human
Happiness is exceeding transient, and, That Death is the certain

End of all Men; the former whereof is inculcated by the fatal End of *Tom Thumb*; the latter, by that of all the other Personages. 110

The *Characters* are, I think, sufficiently described in the *Dramatis Personae*; and I believe we shall find few Plays, where greater care is taken to maintain them throughout, and to preserve in every Speech that Characteristical Mark which distinguishes them from each other. 'But (says Mr. *D*——) how well doth the *Character* of 115 '*Tom Thumb*, whom we must call the Hero of this Tragedy, if it hath 'any Hero, agree with the Precepts of *Aristotle*, who defineth *Tragedy* '*to be the Imitation of a short, but perfect Action, containing a just* '*Greatness in itself*, &c. What Greatness can be in a Fellow, whom History 'relateth to have been no higher than a Span?' This Gentle- 120 man seemeth to think, with Serjeant *Kite*, that the Greatness of a Man's Soul is in proportion to that of his Body, the contrary of which is affirmed by our *English* Physognominical Writers. Besides, if I understand *Aristotle* right, he speaketh only of the Greatness of the Action, and not of the Person. 125

As for the *Sentiments* and the *Diction*, which now only remain to be spoken to; I thought I could afford them no stronger Justification, than by producing parallel Passages out of the best of our *English* Writers. Whether this Sameness of Thought and Expression which I have quoted from them, proceeded from an Agreement in 130 their Way of Thinking; or whether they have borrowed from our Author, I leave the Reader to determine. I shall adventure to affirm this of the Sentiments of our Author; That they are generally the most familiar which I have ever met with, and at the same time delivered with the highest Dignity of Phrase; which brings me to 135 speak of his *Diction*. — Here I shall only beg one Postulatum, *viz*. That the greatest Perfection of the Language of a Tragedy is, that it is not to be understood; which granted (as I think it must be) it will necessarily follow, that the only ways to avoid this, is by being too high or too low for the Understanding, which will comprehend 140 every thing within its Reach. Those two Extremities of Stile Mr. *Dryden* illustrates by the familiar Image of two Inns, which I shall term the Aerial and the Subterrestrial.

Horace goeth farther, and sheweth when it is proper to call at one of these Inns, and when at the other; 145

Telephus & Peleus, cùm pauper & exul uterque,
Projicit Ampullas & Sesquipedalia Verba.

That he approveth of the *Sesquipedalia Verba*, is plain; for had not *Telephus & Peleus* used this sort of Diction in Prosperity, they could not have dropt it in Adversity. The Aerial Inn, therefore (says 150 *Horace*) is proper only to be frequented by Princes and other great Men, in the highest Affluence of Fortune; the Subterrestrial is appointed for the Entertainment of the poorer sort of People only, whom *Horace* advises,

— *dolere Sermone pedestri.* 155

The true Meaning of both which Citations is, That Bombast is the proper Language for Joy, and Doggrel for Grief, the latter of which is literally imply'd in the *Sermo pedestris*, as the former is in the *Sesquipedalia Verba.*

Cicero recommendeth the former of these. *Quid est tam furiosum* 160 *vel tragicum quàm verborum sonitus inanis, nullâ subjectâ Sententiâ neque Scientiâ.* What can be so proper for Tragedy as a Set of big sounding Words, so contrived together, as to convey no Meaning; which I shall one Day or other prove to be the Sublime of *Longinus. Ovid* declareth absolutely for the latter Inn: 165

Omne genus scripti Gravitate Tragaedia vincit.

Tragedy hath of all Writings the greatest Share in the *Bathos*, which is the Profound of *Scriblerus.*

I shall not presume to determine which of these two Stiles be properer for Tragedy. — It sufficeth, that our Author excelleth in 170 both. He is very rarely within sight through the whole Play, either rising higher than the Eye of your Understanding can soar, or sinking lower than it careth to stoop. But here it may perhaps be observed, that I have given more frequent Instances of Authors who have imitated him in the Sublime, than in the contrary. To 175 which I answer, First, Bombast being properly a Redundancy of Genius, Instances of this Nature occur in Poets whose Names do more Honour to our Author, than the Writers in the Doggerel, which proceeds from a cool, calm, weighty Way of Thinking. Instances whereof are most frequently to be found in Authors of a 180 lower Class. Secondly, That the Works of such Authors are difficultly found at all. Thirdly, That it is a very hard Task to read them, in order to extract these Flowers from them. And Lastly, It is very often difficult to transplant them at all; they being like some Flowers of a very nice Nature, which will flourish in no Soil but their own: 185

For it is easy to transcribe a Thought, but not the Want of one. The *Earl of Essex*, for Instance, is a little Garden of choice Rarities, whence you can scarce transplant one Line so as to preserve its original Beauty. This must account to the Reader for his missing the Names of several of his Acquaintance, which he had certainly 190 found here, had I ever read their Works; for which, if I have not a just Esteem, I can at least say with *Cicero*, *Quae non contemno, quippè quae nunquam legerim.* However, that the Reader may meet with due Satisfaction in this Point, I have a young Commentator from the University, who is reading over all the modern Tragedies, 195 at Five Shillings a Dozen, and collecting all that they have stole from our Author, which shall shortly be added as an Appendix to this Work.

DRAMATIS PERSONAE

KING *Arthur*, A passionate sort of King, Husband to Queen *Dollallolla*, of whom he stands a little in Fear; Father to *Huncamunca*, whom he is very fond of; and in Love with *Glumdalca*.	Mr. *Mullart*.
TOM THUMB *the Great*, A little Hero with a great Soul, something violent in his Temper, which is a little abated by his Love for *Huncamunca*.	Young *Verhuyck*.
GHOST of *Gaffar Thumb*, A whimsical sort of Ghost.	Mr. *Lacy*.
Lord GRIZZLE, Extremely zealous for the Liberty of the Subject, very cholerick in his Temper, and in Love with *Huncamunca*. ...	Mr. *Jones*.
MERLIN, A Conjurer, and in some sort Father to *Tom Thumb*.	Mr. *Hallam*.
NOODLE, } Courtiers in Place, and consequently	Mr. *Reynolds*.
DOODLE, } of that Party that is uppermost.	Mr. *Wathan*
FOODLE, A Courtier that is out of Place, and consequently of that Party that is undermost.	Mr. *Ayres*.
BAILIFF, and } Of the Party of the Plaintiff.	Mr. *Peterson*.
FOLLOWER, }	Mr. *Hicks*.
PARSON, Of the Side of the Church.	Mr. *Watson*.

WOMEN

QUEEN *Dollallolla*, Wife to King *Arthur*, and Mother to *Huncamunca*, a Woman entirely faultless, saving that she is a little given to Drink; a little too much a *Virago* towards her Husband, and in Love with *Tom Thumb*. ...	Mrs. *Mullart*.

The Princess HUNCAMUNCA, Daughter to their Majesties King *Arthur* and Queen *Dollallolla*, of a very sweet, gentle, and amorous Disposition, equally in Love with Lord *Grizzle* and *Tom Thumb*, and desirous to be married to them both. … … … … … … … Mrs. *Jones*.

GLUMDALCA, of the Giants, a Captive Queen, belov'd by the King, but in Love with *Tom Thumb*. … … … … … … … … Mrs. *Dove*.

CLEORA,	Maids of Honour, in	*Noodle*.
MUSTACHA,	Love with	*Doodle*.

Courtiers, Guards, Rebels, Drums, Trumpets, Thunder and Lightning.

SCENE *the Court of King* Arthur, *and a Plain thereabouts.*

ACT I

SCENE I

SCENE, *The Palace.*
DOODLE, NOODLE.

DOODLE. Sure, such a [(a)] Day as this was never seen!
The Sun himself, on this auspicious Day,
Shines, like a Beau in a new Birth-Day Suit:
This down the Seams embroider'd, that the Beams.
All Nature wears one universal Grin. 5
NOODLE. This Day, O Mr. *Doodle*, is a Day

(a) *Corneille* recommends some very remarkable Day, wherein to fix the Action of a Tragedy. This the best of our Tragical Writers have understood to mean a Day remarkable for the Serenity of the Sky, or what we generally call a fine Summer's Day: So that according to this their Exposition, the same Months are proper for Tragedy, which are proper for Pastoral. Most 5 of our celebrated *English* Tragedies, as *Cato*, *Mariamne*, *Tamerlane*, &c. begin with their Observations on the Morning. *Lee* seems to have come the nearest to this beautiful Description of our Authors;

The Morning dawns with an unwonted Crimson,
The Flowers all odorous seem, the Garden Birds 10
Sing louder, and the laughing *Sun ascends,*
The gaudy Earth with an unusual brightness,
All Nature smiles. Caes. Borg.

Massinissa in the new *Sophonisba* is also a Favourite of the Sun;

— The Sun too seems 15
As conscious of my Joy with broader Eye
To look abroad the World, and all things smile
Like Sophonisba.

Memnon in the *Persian Princess*, makes the Sun decline rising, that he may not peep on Objects, which would prophane his Brightness. 20

— The Morning rises slow,
And all those ruddy Streaks that us'd to paint
The Days Approach, are lost in Clouds as if
The Horrors of the Night had sent 'em back,
To warn the Sun, he should not leave the Sea, 25
To Peep, &c.

Indeed, [b] a Day we never saw before.
The mighty [c] *Thomas Thumb* victorious comes;
Millions of Giants crowd his Chariot Wheels,
[d] Giants! to whom the Giants in *Guild-hall* 10

---

[b] This Line is highly conformable to the beautiful Simplicity of the Antients. It hath been copied by almost every Modern,

Not to be is not to be in Woe. State of Innocence.
Love is not Sin but where 'tis sinful Love. Don Sebastian.
Nature is Nature, Laelius. Sophonisba. 5
Men are but Men, we did not make our selves. Revenge.

[c] Dr. *B——y* reads the mighty Tall-mast Thumb. Mr. *D——s* the mighty Thumping Thumb. Mr. *T——d* reads Thundering. I think *Thomas* more agreeable to the great Simplicity so apparent in our Author.

[d] That learned Historian Mr. *S——n* in the third Number of his Criticism on our Author, takes great Pains to explode this Passage. It is, says he, difficult to guess what Giants are here meant, unless the Giant *Despair* in the *Pilgrim's Progress*, or the Giant *Greatness* in the *Royal Villain*; for I have heard of no other sort of Giants in the Reign of King *Arthur*. *Petrus* 5 *Burmanus* makes three *Tom Thumbs*, one whereof he supposes to have been the same Person whom the *Greeks* called *Hercules*, and that by these Giants are to be understood the *Centaurs* slain by that Heroe. Another *Tom Thumb* he contends to have been no other than the *Hermes Trismegistus* of the Antients. The third *Tom Thumb* he places under the Reign of King 10 *Arthur*, to which third *Tom Thumb*, says he, the Actions of the other two were attributed. Now tho' I know that this Opinion is supported by an Assertion of *Justus Lipsius*, *Thomam illum Thumbum non alium quam Herculem fuisse satis constat*; yet shall I venture to oppose one Line of Mr. *Midwinter*, against them all, 15

In Arthur's *Court* Tom Thumb *did live.*

But then, says Dr. *B——y*, if we place *Tom Thumb* in the Court of King *Arthur*, it will be proper to place that Court out of *Britain*, where no Giants were ever heard of. *Spencer*, in his *Fairy Queen*, is of another Opinion, where describing *Albion* he says, 20

— Far within a salvage Nation dwelt
Of hideous Giants.

And in the same Canto,

Then Elfar, *who two Brethren Giants had,*
The one of which had two Heads — 25
The other three.

Risum teneatis, Amici.

Are Infant Dwarfs. They frown, and foam, and roar,
While *Thumb* regardless of their Noise rides on.
So some Cock-Sparrow in a Farmer's Yard,
Hops at the Head of an huge Flock of Turkeys.
DOODLE. When Goody *Thumb* first brought this *Thomas* forth, 15
The *Genius* of our Land triumphant reign'd;
Then, then, Oh *Arthur*! did thy *Genius* reign.
NOODLE. They tell me it is [(e)] whisper'd in the Books
Of all our Sages, that this mighty Hero
By *Merlin's* Art begot, hath not a Bone 20
Within his Skin, but is a Lump of Gristle.
DOODLE. Then 'tis a Gristle of no mortal kind,
Some God, my *Noodle*, stept into the Place
Of Gaffer *Thumb*, and more than [(f)] half begot,
This mighty *Tom*. 25
NOODLE. — [(g)] Sure he was sent Express
From Heav'n, to be the Pillar of our State.
Tho' small his Body be, so very small,
A Chairman's Leg is more than twice as large;
Yet is his Soul like any Mountain big, 30

(e) To Whisper in Books says Mr. *D*——*s* is errant Nonsense. I am afraid this learned Man does not sufficiently understand the extensive meaning of the Word Whisper. If he had rightly understood what is meant by the *Senses Whisp'ring the Soul* in the *Persian Princess*, or what *Whisp'ring like Winds* is in *Aurengzebe*, or like Thunder in another Author, he would 5 have understood this. *Emmeline* in *Dryden* sees a Voice, but she was born blind, which is an Excuse *Panthea* cannot plead in *Cyrus*, who hears a sight.

— Your Description will surpass,
All Fiction, Painting, or dumb Shew of Horror, 10
That ever Ears yet heard, or Eyes beheld.

When Mr. *D*——*s* understands these he will understand Whisp'ring in Books.

(f) *— Some Ruffian stept into his Father's Place,*
And more than half begot him. *Mary Q. of Scots.*

(g) *— For* Ulamar *seems* sent Express from Heaven,
To civilize this rugged Indian *Clime.* Liberty Asserted.

And as a Mountain once brought forth a Mouse,
(h) So doth this Mouse contain a mighty Mountain.

DOODLE. Mountain indeed! So terrible his Name,
(i) The Giant Nurses frighten Children with it;
And cry *Tom Thumb* is come, and if you are 35
Naughty, will surely take the Child away.

NOODLE. But hark! (k) these Trumpets speak the King's
Approach.

DOODLE. He comes most luckily for my Petition.

Flourish.

SCENE II

KING, QUEEN, GRIZZLE, NOODLE, DOODLE, FOODLE.

KING. (l) Let nothing but a Face of Joy appear;
The Man who frowns this Day shall lose his Head,

(h) *Omne majus continet in se minus, sed minus non in se majus continere potest,* says *Scaliger* in *Thumbo.* — I suppose he would have cavilled at these beautiful Lines in the Earl of *Essex;*

> — *Thy most inveterate Soul,*
> *That looks through the foul Prison of thy Body.* 5

> And at those of *Dryden,*

> *The Palace is without too well design'd,*
> *Conduct me in, for I will view thy Mind.* Aurengzebe.

(i) Mr. *Banks* hath copied this almost Verbatim,

> *It was enough to say, here's* Essex *come,*
> *And Nurses still'd their Children with the fright.* E. of *Essex.*

(k) The Trumpet in a Tragedy is generally as much as to say enter King: Which makes Mr. *Banks* in one of his Plays call it the Trumpet's formal Sound.

(l) *Phraortes* in the *Captives* seems to have been acquainted with King *Arthur.*

> *Proclaim a Festival for seven Days space,*
> *Let the Court shine in all its Pomp and Lustre,*
> *Let all our Streets resound with Shouts of Joy;*
> *Let Musick's Care-dispelling Voice be heard,* 5
> *The sumptuous Banquet, and the flowing Goblet*
> *Shall warm the Cheek, and fill the Heart with Gladness.*
> *Astarbe shall sit Mistress of the Feast.*

That he may have no Face to frown withal.
Smile, *Dollalolla* — Ha! what wrinkled Sorrow,
(m) Hangs, sits, lies, frowns upon thy knitted Brow? 5
Whence flow those Tears fast down thy blubber'd Cheeks,
Like a swoln Gutter, gushing through the Streets?

QUEEN. (n) Excess of Joy, my Lord, I've heard Folks say,
Gives Tears as certain as Excess of Grief.

KING. If it be so, let all Men cry for Joy, 10
(o) 'Till my whole Court be drowned with their Tears;

(m) *Repentance* frowns *on thy contracted Brow.* Sophonisba.
Hung on his clouded Brow, I mark'd Despair. Ibid.
— A sullen Gloom,
Scowls on his Brow. Busiris.

(n) *Plato* is of this Opinion, and so is Mr. *Banks*;
Behold these Tears sprung from fresh Pain and Joy.
E. of *Essex.*

(o) These Floods are very frequent in the Tragick Authors.
Near to some murmuring Brook I'll lay me down,
Whose Waters if they should too shallow flow,
My Tears shall swell them up till I will drown.
Lee's Sophonisba.

Pouring forth Tears at such a lavish Rate, 5
That were the World on Fire, they might have drown'd
The Wrath of Heav'n, and quench'd the mighty Ruin.
Mithridates.

One Author changes the Waters of Grief to those of Joy,
— These Tears that sprung from Tides of Grief,
Are now augmented to a Flood of Joy. Cyrus the Great. 10

Another,
Turns all the Streams *of Hate, and makes them flow*
In Pity's Channel. Royal Villain.

One drowns himself,
— Pity like a Torrent pours *me down,* 15
Now I am drowning all within a Deluge. Anna Bullen.

Cyrus drowns the whole World,
Our swellin Grief
Shall melt into a Deluge, and the World
Shall drown in Tears. Cyrus the Great. 20

Nay, till they overflow my utmost Land,
And leave me Nothing but the Sea to rule.

DOODLE. My Liege, I a Petition have here got.

KING. Petition me no Petitions, Sir, to-day; 15
Let other Hours be set apart for Business.
To-day it is our Pleasure to be (p) drunk,
And this our Queen shall be as drunk as We.

QUEEN. (Tho' I already (q) half Seas over am)
If the capacious Goblet overflow 20
With *Arrack-Punch* — 'fore *George*! I'll see it out;
Of *Rum*, and *Brandy*, I'll not taste a Drop.

KING. Tho' *Rack*, in *Punch*, Eight Shillings be a Quart,
And *Rum* and *Brandy* be no more than Six,
Rather than quarrel, you shall have your Will. 25

Trumpets.

But, ha! the Warrior comes; the Great *Tom Thumb*;
The little Hero, Giant-killing Boy,
Preserver of my Kingdom, is arrived.

(p) An Expression vastly beneath the Dignity of Tragedy, says Mr. *D——s*, yet we find the Word he cavils at in the Mouth of *Mithridates* less properly used and applied to a more terrible Idea;

I would be drunk with Death. Mithrid.

The Author of the New *Sophonisba* taketh hold of this Monosyllable, and 5
uses it pretty much to the same purpose,

The Carthaginian *Sword with* Roman *Blood*
Was drunk.

I would ask Mr. *D——s* which gives him the best Idea, a drunken King, or a drunken Sword? 10
Mr. *Tate* dresses up King *Arthur's* Resolution in Heroicks,

Merry, my Lord, o'th' Captain's Humour right,
I am resolv'd to be dead drunk to Night.

Lee also uses this charming Word;

Love's the Drunkenness of the Mind. Gloriana. 15

(q) *Dryden* hath borrowed this, and applied it improperly,

I'm half Seas o'er in Death. Cleom.

SCENE III

TOM THUMB, *to them with Officers, Prisoners, and Attendants.*

KING. [r] Oh! welcome most, most welcome to my Arms,
What Gratitude can thank away the Debt,
Your Valour lays upon me?
QUEEN. [*Aside.*] — [s] Oh! ye Gods!
TOM THUMB. When I'm not thank'd at all, I'm thank'd enough, 5
[t] I've done my Duty, and I've done no more.
QUEEN. [*Aside.*] Was ever such a Godlike Creature seen!
KING. Thy Modesty's a [*] Candle to thy Merit,
It shines itself, and shews thy Merit too.
But say, my Boy, where did'st thou leave the Giants? 10
TOM THUMB. My Liege, without the Castle Gates they stand,
The Castle Gates too low for their Admittance.
KING. What look they like?
TOM THUMB. Like Nothing but Themselves.
QUEEN. [u] And sure thou art like nothing but thy Self. 15
KING. [*Aside.*] Enough! the vast Idea fills my Soul.
I see them, yes, I see them now before me:
The monst'rous, ugly, barb'rous Sons of Whores.
But, Ha! what Form Majestick strikes our Eyes?

---

[r] This Figure is in great use among the Tragedians;

'Tis therefore, therefore 'tis. Victim.

I long repent, repent and long again. Busiris.

[s] A Tragical Exclamation.

[t] This Line is copied verbatim in the *Captives.*

[*] We find a Candlestick for this Candle in two celebrated Authors;

— Each Star withdraws
His golden Head and burns within the Socket. Nero.

A Soul grown old and sunk into the Socket. Sebastian.

[u] This Simile occurs very frequently among the Dramatick Writers of both Kinds.

[x] So perfect, that it seems to have been drawn 20
By all the Gods in Council: So fair she is,
That surely at her Birth the Council paus'd,
And then at length cry'd out, This is a Woman!

TOM THUMB. Then were the Gods mistaken. — She is not
A Woman, but a Giantess — whom we 25
[y] With much ado, have made a shift to hawl
Within the Town: [z] for she is by a Foot,
Shorter than all her Subject Giants were.

GLUMDALCA. We yesterday were both a Queen and Wife,
One hundred thousand Giants own'd our Sway, 30
Twenty whereof were married to our self.

QUEEN. Oh! happy State of Giantism — where Husbands
Like Mushrooms grow, whilst hapless we are forc'd
To be content, nay, happy thought with one.

---

[x] Mr. *Lee* hath stolen this Thought from our Author;

— This perfect Face, drawn by the Gods in Council,
Which they were long a making. Lu. Jun. Brut.

— At his Birth, the heavenly Council paus'd,
And then at last cry'd out, This is a Man! 5

Dryden hath improved this Hint to the utmost Perfection:

So perfect, that the very Gods who form'd you, wonder'd
At their own Skill, and cry'd, A lucky Hit
Has mended our Design! Their Envy hindred,
Or you had been Immortal, and a Pattern, 10
When Heaven would work for Ostentation sake,
To copy out again. All for Love.

Banks prefers the Works of *Michael Angelo* to that of the Gods;

A Pattern for the Gods to make a Man by,
Or Michael Angelo *to form a Statue.* 15

[y] It is impossible says Mr. *W*—— sufficiently to admire this natural easy Line.

[z] This Tragedy which in most Points resembles the Antients differs from them in this, that it assigns the same Honour to Lowness of Stature, which they did to Height. The Gods and Heroes in *Homer* and *Virgil* are continually described higher by the Head than their Followers, the contrary of which is observ'd by our Author: In short, to exceed on either 5 side is equally admirable, and a Man of three Foot is as wonderful a sight as a Man of nine.

GLUMDALCA. But then to lose them all in one black Day, 35
That the same Sun, which rising, saw me wife
To Twenty Giants, setting, should behold
Me widow'd of them all. — [(a)] My worn out Heart,
That Ship, leaks fast, and the great heavy Lading,
My Soul, will quickly sink. 40

QUEEN. — Madam, believe,
I view your Sorrows with a Woman's Eye;
But learn to bear them with what Strength you may,
To-morrow we will have our Grenadiers
Drawn out before you, and you then shall choose 45
What Husbands you think fit.

GLUMDALCA. — [(b)] Madam, I am
Your most obedient, and most humble Servant.

KING. Think, mighty Princess, think this Court your own,
Nor think the Landlord me, this House my Inn; 50
Call for whate'er you will, you'll Nothing pay.
[(c)] I feel a sudden Pain within my Breast,
Nor know I whether it arise from Love,
Or only the Wind-Cholick. Time must shew.
Oh *Thumb*! What do we to thy Valour owe? 55
Ask some Reward, great as we can bestow.

TOM THUMB. [(d)] I ask not Kingdoms, I can conquer those,
I ask not Money, Money I've enough;
For what I've done, and what I mean to do,

(a) *My Blood leaks fast, and the great heavy lading*
My Soul will quickly sink. Mithrid.
My Soul is like a Ship. Injur'd Love.

(b) This well-bred Line seems to be copied in the *Persian Princess*;
To be your humblest, and most faithful Slave.

(c) This Doubt of the King puts me in mind of a Passage in the *Captives*, where the Noise of Feet is mistaken for the Rustling of Leaves,
— Methinks I hear
The sound of Feet
No, 'twas the Wind that shook yon Cypress Boughs. 5

(d) Mr. *Dryden* seems to have had this Passage in his Eye in the first Page of *Love Triumphant.*

For Giants slain, and Giants yet unborn, 60
Which I will slay — if this be call'd a Debt,
Take my Receipt in full — I ask but this,
[(e)] To Sun my self in *Huncamunca's* Eyes.

KING. Prodigious bold Request.

QUEEN. [*Aside.*] — [(f)] Be still my Soul. 65

TOM THUMB. [(g)] My Heart is at the Threshold of your Mouth,
And waits its answer there — Oh! do not frown,
I've try'd, to Reason's Tune, to tune my Soul,
But Love did overwind and crack the String.
Tho' *Jove* in Thunder had cry'd out, YOU SHAN'T, 70
I should have lov'd her still — for oh strange fate,
Then when I lov'd her least, I lov'd her most.

KING. It is resolv'd — the Princess is your own.

TOM THUMB. [(h)] Oh! happy, happy, happy, happy, *Thumb*!

QUEEN. Consider, Sir, reward your Soldiers Merit, 75
But give not *Huncamunca* to *Tom Thumb*.

KING. *Tom Thumb*! Odzooks, my wide extended Realm
Knows not a Name so glorious as *Tom Thumb*.
Let *Macedonia*, *Alexander* boast,

(e) *Don Carlos* in the Revenge suns himself in the Charms of his Mistress,

While in the Lustre of her Charms I lay.

(f) A Tragical Phrase much in use.

(g) This Speech hath been taken to pieces by several Tragical Authors who seem to have rifled it and shared its Beauties among them.

My soul waits at the Portal of thy Breast,
To ravish from thy Lips the welcome News. Anna Bullen.

My Soul stands listening at my Ears. Cyrus the Great. 5

Love to his Tune my jarring Heart would bring,
But Reason overwinds and cracks the String. D. of Guise.

— I should have lov'd,
Tho' Jove *in* muttering *Thunder had forbid it.*
New Sophonisba.

And when it (my Heart) *wild resolves to love no more,* 10
Then is the Triumph of excessive Love. Ibidem.

(h) *Massinissa* is one fourth less happy than *Tom Thumb*.

Oh! happy, happy, happy. New Sophonisba.

Let *Rome* her *Caesar's* and her *Scipio's* show, 80
Her Messieurs *France*, let *Holland* boast *Mynheers*,
Ireland her O's, her *Mac's* let *Scotland* boast,
Let *England* boast no other than *Tom Thumb*.

QUEEN. Tho' greater yet his boasted Merit was,
He shall not have my Daughter, that is Pos'. 85

KING. Ha! sayst thou *Dollalolla?*

QUEEN. — I say he shan't.

KING. (i) Then by our Royal Self we swear you lye.

QUEEN. (k) Who but a Dog, who but a Dog,
Would use me as thou dost? Me, who have lain 90
(l) These twenty Years so loving by thy Side.
But I will be reveng'd. I'll hang my self,
Then tremble all who did this Match persuade,
(m) For riding on a Cat, from high I'll fall,
And squirt down Royal Vengeance on you all. 95

FOODLE. (n) Her Majesty the Queen is in a Passion.

KING. (o) Be she, or be she not — I'll to the Girl
And pave thy Way, oh *Thumb* — Now, by our self,
We were indeed a pretty King of Clouts,
To truckle to her Will — For when by Force 100
Or Art the Wife her Husband over-reaches,
Give him the Peticoat, and her the Breeches.

(i) *No by my self.* Anna Bullen.

(k) *— Who caus'd,*
This dreadful Revolution in my Fate?
Ulamar. *Who but a Dog, who but a Dog?*
Liberty Asserted.

(l) *— A Bride,*
Who twenty Years lay loving *by your Side.* Banks.

(m) *For born upon a Cloud, from high I'll fall,*
And rain down Royal Vengeance on you all.
Albion Queens.

(n) An Information very like this we have in the *Tragedy of Love*, where *Cyrus* having stormed in the most violent manner, *Cyaxares* observes very calmly,

Why, Nephew Cyrus — *you are mov'd.*

(o) *'Tis in your Choice,*
Love me, or love me not! Conquest of Granada.

TOM THUMB. [p] Whisper, ye Winds, that *Huncamunca's* mine;
Echoes repeat, that *Huncamunca's* mine!
The dreadful Bus'ness of the War is o'er, 105
And Beauty, heav'nly Beauty! crowns my Toils,
I've thrown the bloody Garment now aside,
And *Hymeneal* Sweets invite my Bride.
So when some Chimney-Sweeper, all the Day,
Hath through dark Paths pursu'd the sooty Way, 110
At Night, to wash his Hands and Face he flies,
And in his t'other Shirt with his *Brickdusta* lies.

SCENE IV

GRIZZLE *solus.*

GRIZZLE. [q] Where art thou *Grizzle*? where are now thy Glories?
Where are the Drums that waken'd thee to Honour?
Greatness is a lac'd Coat from *Monmouth-Street*,
Which Fortune lends us for a Day to wear,
To-morrow puts it on another's Back. 5
The spiteful Sun but yesterday survey'd
His Rival, high as Saint *Paul's* Cupola;
Now may he see me as *Fleet-Ditch* laid low.

SCENE V

QUEEN, GRIZZLE.

QUEEN. [r] Teach me to scold, prodigious-minded *Grizzle.*
Mountain of Treason, ugly as the Devil,
Teach this confounded hateful Mouth of mine,

---

[p] There is not one Beauty in this Charming Speech, but hath been borrowed by almost every Tragick Writer.

[q] Mr. *Banks* has (I wish I could not say too servilely) imitated this of *Grizzle* in his *Earl of Essex.*

Where art thou Essex, &c.

[r] The Countess of *Nottingham* in the *Earl of Essex* is apparently acquainted with *Dollalolla.*

To spout forth Words malicious as thy self,
Words, which might shame all *Billingsgate* to speak. 5

GRIZZLE. Far be it from my Pride, to think my Tongue
Your Royal Lips can in that Art instruct,
Wherein you so excel. But may I ask,
Without Offence, wherefore my Queen would scold?

QUEEN. Wherefore, Oh! Blood and Thunder! han't you heard 10
(What ev'ry Corner of the Court resounds)
That little *Thumb* will be a great Man made.

GRIZZLE. I heard it, I confess — for who, alas!
(s) Can always stop his Ears — but wou'd my Teeth,
By grinding Knives, had first been set on Edge. 15

QUEEN. Would I had heard at the still Noon of Night,
The Hallaloo of Fire in every Street!
Odsbobs! I have a mind to hang my self,
To think I shou'd a Grandmother be made
By such a Raskal. — Sure the King forgets, 20
When in a Pudding, by his Mother put,
The Bastard, by a Tinker, on a Stile
Was drop'd. — O, good Lord *Grizzle*! can I bear
To see him from a Pudding, mount the Throne?
Or can, Oh can! my *Huncamunca* bear, 25
To take a Pudding's Offspring to her Arms?

GRIZZLE. Oh Horror! Horror! Horror! cease my Queen,
(t) Thy Voice like twenty Screech-Owls, wracks my Brain.

QUEEN. Then rouse thy Spirit — we may yet prevent
This hated Match .— 30

GRIZZLE. — We will; (u) not Fate it self,
Should it conspire with *Thomas Thumb*, should cause it.
I'll swim through Seas; I'll ride upon the Clouds;
I'll dig the Earth; I'll blow out ev'ry Fire;

(s) *Grizzle* was not probably possessed of that Glew, of which Mr. *Banks* speaks in his *Cyrus.*

I'll glew my Ears to ev'ry word.

(t) *Screech-Owls, dark Ravens and amphibious Monsters,*
Are screaming in that Voice. Mary Q. of Scots.

(u) The Reader may see all the Beauties of this Speech in a late Ode called the *Naval Lyrick.*

I'll rave; I'll rant; I'll rise; I'll rush; I'll roar; 35
Fierce as the Man whom [x] smiling Dolphins bore,
From the Prosaick to Poetick Shore.
I'll tear the Scoundrel into twenty Pieces.

QUEEN. Oh, no! prevent the Match, but hurt him not;
For, tho' I would not have him have my Daughter, 40
Yet can we kill the Man that kill'd the Giants?

GRIZZLE. I tell you, Madam, it was all a Trick,
He made the Giants first, and then he kill'd them;
As Fox-hunters bring Foxes to the Wood,
And then with Hounds they drive them out again. 45

QUEEN. How! have you seen no Giants? Are there not
Now, in the Yard, ten thousand proper Giants?

GRIZZLE. [y] Indeed, I cannot positively tell,
But firmly do believe there is not One.

QUEEN. Hence! from my Sight! thou Traitor, hie away; 50
By all my Stars! thou enviest *Tom Thumb*.
Go, Sirrah! go, [z] hie away! hie! — thou art

---

[x] This Epithet to a Dolphin doth not give one so clear an Idea as were to be wished, a smiling Fish seeming a little more difficult to be imagined than a flying Fish. Mr. *Dryden* is of Opinion, that smiling is the Property of Reason, and that no irrational Creature can smile.

Smiles not allowed to Beasts from Reason move. 5
State of Innocence.

[y] These Lines are written in the same Key with those in the *Earl of Essex*;

Why sayst thou so, I love thee well, indeed
I do, and thou shalt find by this, 'tis true.

Or with this in *Cyrus*;

The most heroick Mind that ever was. 5

And with above half of the modern Tragedies.

[z] *Aristotle* in that excellent Work of his which is very justly stiled his Master-piece, earnestly recommends using the Terms of Art, however coarse or even indecent they may be. Mr. *Tate* is of the same Opinion.

Bru. *Do not, like young Hawks, fetch a Course about,*
Your Game flies fair. 5
Fra. *Do not fear it.*
He answers you in your own *Hawking Phrase.*
Injur'd Love.

A setting Dog, be gone.
GRIZZLE. Madam, I go.
Tom Thumb shall feel the Vengeance you have rais'd: 55
So, when two Dogs are fighting in the Streets,
With a third Dog, one of the two Dogs meets,
With angry Teeth, he bites him to the Bone,
And this Dog smarts for what that Dog had done.

SCENE VI

QUEEN *sola.*

QUEEN. And whither shall I go? — Alack-a-day!
I love *Tom Thumb* — but must not tell him so;
For what's a Woman, when her Virtue's gone?
A Coat without its Lace; Wig out of Buckle;
A Stocking with a Hole in't — I can't live 5
Without my Virtue, or without *Tom Thumb.*
(zz) Then let me weigh them in two equal Scales,
In this Scale put my Virtue, that, *Tom Thumb.*
Alas! *Tom Thumb* is heavier than my Virtue.
But hold! — perhaps I may be left a Widow: 10
This Match prevented, then *Tom Thumb* is mine:
In that dear Hope, I will forget my Pain.
So, when some Wench to *Tothill-Bridewell's* sent,
With beating Hemp, and Flogging she's content:
She hopes in time to ease her present Pain, 15
At length is free, and walks the Streets again.

THE END OF THE FIRST ACT.

I think these two great Authorities are sufficient to justify *Dollalolla* in the use of the Phrase — *Hie away hie*; when in the same Line she says she is speaking to a setting Dog. 10

(zz) We meet with such another Pair of Scales in *Dryden's* King *Arthur.*

Arthur *and* Oswald *and their different Fates,*
Are weighing now within the Scales of Heav'n

Also in *Sebastian.*

This Hour my Lot is weighing in the Scales. 5

ACT II

SCENE I

SCENE, *The Street.*
BAILIFF, FOLLOWER.

BAILIFF. Come on, my trusty Follower, come on,
This Day discharge thy Duty, and at Night
A Double Mug of Beer, and Beer shall glad thee.
Stand here by me, this Way must *Noodle* pass.
FOLLOWER. No more, no more, Oh Bailiff! every Word 5
Inspires my Soul with Virtue. — Oh! I long
To meet the Enemy in the Street — and nab him;
To lay arresting Hands upon his Back,
And drag him trembling to the Spunging-House.
BAILIFF. There, when I have him, I will spunge upon him. 10
[a] Oh! glorious Thought! by the Sun, Moon, and Stars,
I will enjoy it, tho it be in Thought!
Yes, yes, my Follower, I will enjoy it.
FOLLOWER. Enjoy it then some other time, for now
Our Prey approaches. 15
BAILIFF. Let us retire.

SCENE II

TOM THUMB, NOODLE, BAILIFF, FOLLOWER.

TOM THUMB. Trust me my *Noodle*, I am wondrous sick;
For tho' I love the gentle *Huncamunca*,
Yet at the Thought of Marriage, I grow pale;

---

[a] Mr. *Rowe* is generally imagin'd to have taken some Hints from this Scene in his Character of *Bajazet*; but as he, of all the Tragick Writers, bears the least Resemblance to our Author in his Diction, I am unwilling to imagine he would condescend to copy him in this Particular.

For Oh! — [b] but swear thoul't keep it ever secret,
I will unfold a Tale will make thee stare. 5

NOODLE. I swear by lovely *Huncamunca's* Charms.

TOM THUMB. Then know — [c] my Grand-mamma hath often said,
Tom Thumb, beware of Marriage.

NOODLE. Sir, I blush
To think a Warrior great in Arms as you, 10
Should be affrighted by his Grand-mamma;
Can an old Woman's empty Dreams deter
The blooming Hero from the Virgin's Arms?
Think of the Joy that will your Soul alarm,
When in her fond Embraces clasp'd you lie, 15
While on her panting Breast dissolv'd in Bliss,
You pour out all *Tom Thumb* in every Kiss.

TOM THUMB. Oh! *Noodle*, thou hast fir'd my eager Soul;
Spight of my Grandmother, she shall be mine;
I'll hug, caress, I'll eat her up with Love. 20
Whole Days, and Nights, and Years shall be too short
For our Enjoyment, every Sun shall rise
[d] Blushing, to see us in our Bed together.

---

[b] This Method of surprizing an Audience by raising their Expectation to the highest Pitch, and then baulking it, hath been practis'd with great Success by most of our Tragical Authors.

[c] *Almeyda* in *Sebastian* is in the same Distress;

> *Sometimes methinks I hear the Groan of Ghosts,*
> *Thin hollow Sounds and lamentable Screams;*
> *Then, like a dying Echo from afar,*
> *My Mother's Voice that cries, wed not* Almeyda
> *Forewarn'd,* Almeyda, *Marriage is thy Crime.*

[d] As very well he may if he hath any Modesty in him, says Mr. *D——s.* The Author of *Busiris*, is extremely zealous to prevent the Sun's blushing at any indecent Object; and therefore on all such Occasions he addresses himself to the Sun, and desires him to keep out of the way.

> *Rise never more, O Sun! let Night prevail,* 5
> *Eternal Darkness close the World's wide Scene.* Busiris.
> *Sun hide thy Face and put the World in Mourning.* Ibid.

NOODLE. Oh Sir! this Purpose of your Soul pursue.
BAILIFF. Oh, Sir! I have an Action against you. 25
NOODLE. At whose Suit is it?
BAILIFF. At your Taylor's, Sir.
Your Taylor put this Warrant in my Hands,
And I arrest you, Sir, at his Commands.
TOM THUMB. Ha! Dogs! Arrest my Friend before my Face! 30
Think you *Tom Thumb* will suffer this Disgrace!
But let vain Cowards threaten by their Word,
Tom Thumb shall shew his Anger by his Sword.

Kills the BAILIFF *and his* FOLLOWER.

BAILIFF. Oh, I am slain!
FOLLOWER. I am murthered also, 35
And to the Shades, the dismal Shades below,
My Bailiff's faithful Follower I go.
NOODLE. (e) Go then to Hell, like Rascals as you are,
And give our Service to the Bailiffs there.
TOM THUMB. Thus perish all the Bailiffs in the Land, 40
Till Debtors at Noon-Day shall walk the Streets,
And no one fear a Bailiff or his Writ.

SCENE III

The Princess Huncamunca's *Apartment.*
HUNCAMUNCA, CLEORA, MUSTACHA.

HUNCAMUNCA. (f) Give me some Musick — see that it be sad.
CLEORA *sings.*

Mr. *Banks* makes the Sun perform the Office of *Hymen*; and therefore not likely to be disgusted at such a Sight;

The Sun sets forth like a gay Brideman with you. 10
Mary Q. of Scots.

(e) *Nourmahal* sends the same Message to Heaven;

For I would have you, when you upwards move,
Speak kindly of us, to our Friends above. Aurengzebe.

We find another to Hell, in the *Persian* Princess;

Villain, get thee down 5
To Hell, and tell them that the Fray's begun.

(f) *Anthony* gives the same Command in the same Words.

Cupid, *ease a Love-sick Maid,*
Bring thy Quiver to her Aid;
With equal Ardor wound the Swain:
Beauty should never sigh in vain. 5

II.

Let him feel the pleasing Smart,
Drive thy Arrow thro' his Heart;
When One you wound, you then destroy;
When Both you kill, you kill with Joy.

HUNCAMUNCA. [g] O, *Tom Thumb*! *Tom Thumb*! wherefore art thou *Tom Thumb*? 10
Why had'st thou not been born of Royal Race?
Why had not mighty *Bantam* been thy Father?
Or else the King of *Brentford*, *Old* or *New*?

MUSTACHA. I am surpriz'd that your Highness can give your self a Moment's Uneasiness about that little insignificant Fellow, 15 [h] *Tom Thumb the Great* — One properer for a Play-thing, than a Husband. — Were he my Husband, his Horns should be as long as his Body. — If you had fallen in Love with a Grenadier, I should not have wonder'd at it — If you had fallen in Love with Something; but to fall in Love with Nothing! 20

HUNCAMUNCA. Cease, my *Mustacha*, on thy Duty cease.
The *Zephyr*, when in flowry Vales it plays,
Is not so soft, so sweet as *Thummy's* Breath.
The Dove is not so gentle to its Mate.

MUSTACHA. The Dove is every bit as proper for a Husband — 25 Alas! Madam, there's not a Beau about the Court looks so little like a Man — He is a perfect Butterfly, a Thing without Substance, and almost without Shadow too.

HUNCAMUNCA. This Rudeness is unseasonable, desist;
Or, I shall think this Railing comes from Love. 30

---

[g] Oh! *Marius, Marius*; wherefore art thou *Marius*? Otway's Marius.

[h] Nothing is more common than these seeming Contradictions; such as,

Haughty Weakness. Victim.
Great small World. Noah's Flood.

Tom Thumb's a Creature of that charming Form,
That no one can abuse, unless they love him.
MUSTACHA. Madam, the King.

SCENE IV

KING, HUNCAMUNCA.

KING. Let all but *Huncamunca* leave the Room.

Exit CLEORA, *and* MUSTACHA.

Daughter, I have observ'd of late some Grief,
Unusual in your Countenance — your Eyes,
(i) That, like two open Windows, us'd to shew
The lovely Beauty of the Rooms within, 5
Have now two Blinds before them — What is the Cause?
Say, have you not enough of Meat and Drink?
We've giv'n strict Orders not to have you stinted.
HUNCAMUNCA. Alas! my Lord, I value not my self,
That once I eat two Fowls and half a Pig; 10
(k) Small is that Praise; but oh! a Maid may want,
What she can neither eat nor drink.

(i) *Lee* hath improv'd this Metaphor.

Dost thou not view Joy peeping from my Eyes,
The Casements open'd wide to gaze on thee;
So Rome's *glad Citizens to Windows rise,*
When they some young Triumpher fain would see. Gloriana. 5

(k) *Almahide* hath the same Contempt for these Appetites;

To eat and drink can no Perfection be. Conquest of Granada.

The Earl of *Essex* is of a different Opinion, and seems to place the chief Happiness of a General therein.

Were but Commanders half so well rewarded, 5
Then they might eat. Banks' Earl of Essex.

But if we may believe one, who knows more than either, the Devil himself; we shall find Eating to be an Affair of more moment than is generally imagined.

Gods are immortal only by their Food. 10
Lucifer in the State of Innocence.

KING. What's that?
HUNCAMUNCA. (l) O spare my Blushes; but I mean a Husband.
KING. If that be all, I have provided one, 15
A Husband great in Arms, whose warlike Sword
Streams with the yellow Blood of slaughter'd Giants.
Whose Name in *Terrâ Incognitâ* is known,
Whose Valour, Wisdom, Virtue make a Noise,
Great as the Kettle-Drums of twenty Armies. 20
HINCAMUNCA. Whom does my Royal Father mean?
KING. *Tom Thumb.*
HUNCAMUNCA. Is it possible?
KING. Ha! the Window-Blinds are gone,
(m) A Country Dance of Joy is in your Face, 25
Your Eyes spit Fire, your Cheeks grow red as Beef.
HUNCAMUNCA. O, there's a Magick-musick in that Sound,
Enough to turn me into Beef indeed.
Yes, I will own, since licens'd by your Word,
I'll own *Tom Thumb* the Cause of all my Grief. 30
For him I've sigh'd, I've wept, I've gnaw'd my Sheets.
KING. Oh! thou shalt gnaw thy tender Sheets no more,
A Husband thou shalt have to mumble now.
HUNCAMUNCA. Oh! happy Sound! henceforth, let no one tell,
That *Huncamunca* shall lead Apes in Hell. 35
Oh! I am over-joy'd!

(l) This Expression is enough of it self (says Mr. *D——s*) utterly to destroy the Character of *Huncamunca*; yet we find a Woman of no abandon'd Character in *Dryden*, adventuring farther and thus excusing her self;

To speak our Wishes first, forbid it Pride,
Forbid it Modesty: True, they forbid it, 5
But Nature does not, when we are athirst,
Or hungry, will imperious Nature stay,
Nor eat, nor drink, before 'tis bid fall on. Cleomenes.

Cassandra speaks before she is asked. *Huncamunca* afterwards.
Cassandra speaks her Wishes to her Lover. 10
Huncamunca *only to her Father.*

(m) *Her Eyes resistless Magick bear,*
Angels I see, and Gods are dancing there.
Lee's Sophonisba.

KING. I see thou art.
[n]Joy lightens in thy Eyes, and thunders from thy Brows;
Transports, like Lightning, dart along thy Soul,
As Small-shot thro' a Hedge. 40
HUNCAMUNCA. Oh! say not small.
KING. This happy News shall on our Tongue ride Post,
Our self will bear the happy News to *Thumb*.
Yet think not, Daughter, that your powerful Charms
Must still detain the Hero from his Arms; 45
Various his Duty, various his Delight;
Now is his Turn to kiss, and now to fight;
And now to kiss again. So, mighty [o]*Jove*,
When with excessive thund'ring tir'd above,
Comes down to Earth, and takes a Bit — and then, 50
Flies to his Trade of Thund'ring, back again.

SCENE V

GRIZZLE, HUNCAMUNCA.

[p]GRIZZLE. Oh! *Huncamunca*, *Huncamunca*, oh,
Thy pouting Breasts, like Kettle-Drums of Brass,

---

[n] Mr. *Dennis* in that excellent Tragedy, call'd *Liberty Asserted*, which is thought to have given so great a Stroke to the late *French* King, hath frequent Imitations of this beautiful Speech of King *Arthur*;

Conquest light'ning in his Eyes, and thund'ring in his Arm.
Joy lighten'd in her Eyes. 5
Joys like Light'ning dart along my Soul.

[o] Jove *with excessive Thund'ring tir'd above,*
Comes down for Ease, enjoys a Nymph, and then
Mounts dreadful, and to Thund'ring goes again. Gloriana.

[p] This beautiful Line, which ought, says Mr. *W*—— to be written in Gold, is imitated in the New *Sophonisba*;

Oh! *Sophonisba*, *Sophonisba*, oh!
Oh! *Narva*, *Narva*, oh!

The Author of a Song call'd Duke upon Duke, hath improv'd it. 5

Alas! O Nick, O Nick, *alas!*

Where, by the help of a little false Spelling, you have two Meanings in the repeated Words.

Beat everlasting loud Alarms of Joy;
As bright as Brass they are, and oh, as hard;
Oh *Huncamunca*, *Huncamunca*! oh! 5

HUNCAMUNCA. Ha! do'st thou know me, Princess as I am,
*That thus of me you dare to make your Game.

GRIZZLE. Oh *Huncamunca*, well I know that you
A Princess are, and a King's Daughter too.
But Love no Meanness scorns, no Grandeur fears, 10
Love often Lords into the Cellar bears,
And bids the sturdy Porter come up Stairs.
For what's too high for Love, or what's too low?
Oh *Huncamunca*, *Huncamunca*, oh!

HUNCAMUNCA. But granting all you say of Love were true, 15
My Love, alas! is to another due!
In vain to me, a Suitoring you come;
For I'm already promis'd to *Tom Thumb*.

GRIZZLE. And can my Princess such a Durgen wed,
One fitter for your Pocket than your Bed! 20
Advis'd by me, the worthless Baby shun,
Or you will ne'er be brought to bed of one.
Oh take me to thy Arms and never flinch,
Who am a Man by *Jupiter* ev'ry Inch.
(q) Then while in Joys together lost we lie 25
I'll press thy Soul while Gods stand wishing by.

HUNCAMUNCA. If, Sir, what you insinuate you prove
All Obstacles of Promise you remove;
For all Engagements to a Man must fall,
Whene'er that Man is prov'd no Man at all. 30

GRIZZLE. Oh let him seek some Dwarf, some fairy Miss,
Where no Joint-stool must lift him to the Kiss.
But by the Stars and Glory, you appear
Much fitter for a *Prussian* Grenadier;

---

* *Edith*, in the *Bloody Brother*, speaks to her Lover in the same familiar Language.

Your Grace is full of Game.

(q) *Traverse the glitt'ring Chambers of the Sky,*
Born on a Cloud in view of Fate I'll lie,
And press her Soul while Gods stand wishing by. Hannibal.

One Globe alone, on *Atlas* Shoulders rests, 35
Two Globes are less than *Huncamunca's* Breasts:
The Milky-way is not so white, that's flat,
And sure thy Breasts are full as large as that.

HUNCAMUNCA. Oh, Sir, so strong your Eloquence I find,
It is impossible to be unkind. 40

GRIZZLE. Ah! speak that o'er again, and let the (r) Sound
From one Pole to another Pole rebound;
The Earth and Sky, each be a Battledoor
And keep the Sound, that Shuttlecock, up an Hour;
To *Doctors Commons*, for a License I, 45
Swift as an Arrow from a Bow will fly.

HUNCAMUNCA. Oh no! lest some Disaster we should meet,
'Twere better to be marry'd at the Fleet.

GRIZZLE. Forbid it, all ye Powers, a Princess should
By that vile Place, contaminate her Blood; 50
My quick Return shall to my Charmer prove,
I travel on the (s) Post-Horses of Love.

HUNCAMUNCA. Those Post-Horses to me will seem too slow,
Tho' they should fly swift as the Gods, when they
Ride on behind that Post-Boy, Opportunity. 55

SCENE VI

TOM THUMB, HUNCAMUNCA.

TOM THUMB. Where is my Princess, where's my *Huncamunca*?
Where are those Eyes, those Cardmatches of Love,

(r) *Let the four Winds from distant Corners meet,*
And on their Wings first bear it into France;
Then back again to Edina's *proud Walls,*
Till Victim to the Sound th' aspiring City falls.
Albion Queens.

(s) I do not remember any Metaphors so frequent in the Tragick Poets as those borrow'd from Riding Post;

The Gods and Opportunity ride Post. Hannibal.

— Let's rush together,
For Death rides Post. Duke of Guise. 5

Destruction gallops to thy murther Post. Gloriana.

That [t] Light up all with Love my waxen Soul?
Where is that Face which artful Nature made
[u] In the same Moulds where *Venus* self was cast? 5

---

[t] This Image too very often occurs;

— Bright as when thy Eye
'First lighted up our Loves. Aurengzebe.

This not a Crown alone lights up my Name. Busiris.

[u] There is great Dissension among the Poets concerning the Method of making Man. One tells his Mistress that the Mold she was made in being lost, Heaven cannot form such another. *Lucifer*, in *Dryden*, gives a merry Description of his own Formation;

Whom Heaven neglecting, made and scarce design'd, 5
But threw me in for Number to the rest. State of Innocence.

In one Place, the same Poet supposes Man to be made of Metal;

I was form'd
Of that coarse Metal, which when she was made,
The Gods threw by for Rubbish. All for Love. 10

In another, of Dough;

When the Gods moulded up the Paste of Man,
Some of their Clay was left upon their Hands,
And so they made Egyptians. Cleomenes.

In another of Clay; 15

— Rubbish of remaining Clay. Sebastian.

One makes the Soul of Wax;

Her waxen Soul begins to melt apace. Anna Bullen.

Another of Flint;

Sure our two Souls have somewhere been acquainted 20
In former Beings, or struck out together,
One Spark to Africk *flew, and one to* Portugal. Sebastian

To omit the great Quantities of Iron, Brazen and Leaden Souls which are so plenty in modern Authors—I cannot omit the Dress of a Soul as we find it in *Dryden*; 25

Souls shirted but with Air. King Arthur.

Nor can I pass by a particular sort of Soul in a particular sort of Description, in the New *Sophonisba*.

Ye mysterious Powers,
— Whether thro' your gloomy Depths I wander, 30
Or on the Mountains walk; give me the calm,
The steady smiling Soul, where Wisdom sheds
Eternal Sun-shine, and eternal Joy.

HUNCAMUNCA. [x]Oh! What is Musick to the Ear that's deaf,
Or a Goose-Pye to him that has no taste?
What are these Praises now to me, since I
Am promis'd to another?
TOM THUMB. Ha! promis'd. 10
HUNCAMUNCA. Too sure; it's written in the Book of Fate.
TOM THUMB. [y]Then I will tear away the Leaf
Wherein it's writ, or if Fate won't allow
So large a Gap within its Journal-Book,
I'll blot it out at least. 15

SCENE VII

GLUMDALCA, TOM THUMB, HUNCAMUNCA.

GLUMDALCA. [z]I need not ask if you are *Huncamunca*,
Your Brandy Nose proclaims —
HUNCAMUNCA. I am a Princess;
Nor need I ask who you are.
GLUMDALCA. A Giantess; 5
The Queen of those who made and unmade Queens.
HUNCAMUNCA. The Man, whose chief Ambition is to be
My Sweetheart, hath destroy'd these mighty Giants.
GLUMDALCA. Your Sweetheart? do'st thou think the Man, who once
Hath worn my easy Chains, will e'er wear thine? 10
HUNCAMUNCA. Well may your Chains be easy, since if Fame

---

[x] This Line Mr. *Banks* has plunder'd entire in his *Anna Bullen.*

[y] *Good Heaven, the Book of Fate before me lay,*
But to tear out the Journal of that Day.
Or if the Order of the World below,
Will not the Gap of one whole Day allow,
Give me that Minute when she made her Vow. 5

Conquest of Granada.

[z] I know some of the Commentators have imagined, that Mr. *Dryden*, in the *Altercative* Scene between *Cleopatra* and *Octavia*, a Scene which Mr. *Addison* inveighs against with great Bitterness, is much beholden to our Author. How just this their Observation is, I will not presume to determine.

Says true, they have been try'd on twenty Husbands.
[zz] The Glove or Boot, so many times pull'd on,
May well sit easy on the Hand or Foot.
GLUMDALCA. I glory in the Number, and when I 15
Sit poorly down, like thee, content with one,
Heaven change this Face for one as bad as thine.
HUNCAMUNCA. Let me see nearer what this Beauty is,
That captivates the Heart of Men by Scores.

Holds a Candle to her Face.

Oh! Heaven, thou art as ugly as the Devil. 20
GLUMDALCA. You'd give the best of Shoes within your Shop,
To be but half so handsome.
HUNCAMUNCA. — Since you come
[a] To that, I'll put my Beauty to the Test;
Tom Thumb, I'm yours, if you with me will go. 25
GLUMDALCA. Oh! stay, *Tom Thumb*, and you alone shall fill
That Bed where twenty Giants us'd to lie.
TOM THUMB. In the Balcony that o'er-hangs the Stage,
I've seen a Whore two 'Prentices engage;
One half a Crown does in his Fingers hold, 30
The other shews a little Piece of Gold;
She the Half Guinea wisely does purloin,
And leaves the larger and the baser Coin.

Exeunt all but GLUMDALCA.

[zz] A cobling Poet indeed, says Mr. *D.* and yet I believe we may find as monstrous Images in the Tragick-Authors: I'll put down one;

Untie your folded Thoughts, and let them dangle loose as a
Bride's Hair. Injur'd Love.

Which Lines seem to have as much Title to a Milliner's Shop, as our 5
Author's to a Shoemaker's.

[a] Mr. *L*—— takes occasion in this Place to commend the great Care of our Author to preserve the Metre of Blank Verse, in which *Shakespear*, *Johnson* and *Fletcher* were so notoriously negligent; and the Moderns, in Imitation of our Author, so laudably observant;

— Then does 5
Your Majesty believe that he can be
A Traitor! Earl of Essex.

Every Page of *Sophonisba* gives us Instances of this Excellence.

GLUMDALCA. Left, scorn'd, and loath'd for such a Chit as this;
[b] I feel the Storm that's rising in my Mind, 35
Tempests, and Whirlwinds rise, and rowl and roar.
I'm all within a Hurricane, as if
[c] The World's four Winds were pent within my Carcass.
[d] Confusion, Horror, Murder, Guts and Death.

SCENE VIII

KING, GLUMDALCA.

KING. * Sure never was so sad a King as I,
[e] My Life is worn as ragged as a Coat
A Beggar wears; a Prince should put it off,
[f] To love a Captive and a Giantess.
Oh Love! Oh Love! how great a King art thou!
My Tongue's thy Trumpet, and thou Trumpetest,
Unknown to me, within me. [g] oh *Glumdalca*!
Heaven thee design'd a Giantess to make,
But an Angelick Soul was shuffled in.

---

[b] *Love mounts and rowls about my stormy Mind.* Aurengzebe.
Tempests and Whirlwinds thro' my Bosom move. Cleom.

[c] *With such a furious Tempest on his Brow,*
As if the World's four Winds were pent within
His blustring Carcase. Anna Bullen.

[d] Verba Tragica.

* This Speech hath been terribly maul'd by the Poets.

[e] *— My Life is worn to Rags;*
Not worth a Prince's wearing. Love Triumph.

[f] *Must I beg the Pity of my Slave?*
Must a King beg! But Love's a greater King,
A Tyrant, nay a Devil that possesses me.
He tunes the Organ of my Voice and speaks,
Unknown to me, within me. Sebastian. 5

[g] *When thou wer't form'd, Heaven did a Man begin;*
But a Brute Soul by chance was shuffled in. Aurengzebe.

(h) I am a Multitude of Walking Griefs, 10
And only on her Lips the Balm is found,
(i) To spread a Plaister that might cure them all.
GLUMDALCA. What do I hear?
KING. What do I see?
GLUMDALCA. Oh! 15
KING. Ah!
(k) GLUMDALCA. Ah Wretched Queen!
KING. Oh! Wretched King!
GLUMDALCA. Ah!
KING. (l) Oh! 20

SCENE IX

TOM THUMB, HUNCAMUNCA, PARSON.

PARSON. Happy's the Wooing, that's not long adoing;
For if I guess aright, *Tom Thumb* this Night
Shall give a Being to a New *Tom Thumb*.

(h) *— I am a Multitude,*
Of walking Griefs. New Sophonisba.

(i) *I will take thy Scorpion Blood,*
And lay it to my Grief till I have Ease. Anna Bullen.

(k) Our Author, who every where shews his great Penetration into human Nature, here outdoes himself: Where a less judicious Poet would have raised a long Scene of whining Love. He who understood the Passions better, and that so violent an Affection as this must be too big for Utterance, chooses rather to send his Characters off in this sullen and doleful manner: 5
In which admirable Conduct he is imitated by the Author of the justly celebrated *Eurydice*. Dr. *Young* seems to point at this Violence of Passion;

— Passion choaks
Their Words, and they're the Statues of Despair.

And *Seneca* tells us, *Curaeleves Loquuntur, ingentes stupent*. The Story of the 10
Egyptian King in *Herodotus* is too well known to need to be inserted; I refer the more curious Reader to the excellent *Montagne*, who hath written an Essay on this Subject.

(l) *To part is Death —*
— 'Tis Death to part.
— Ah.
— Oh. Don Carlos.

TOM THUMB. It shall be my Endeavour so to do.
HUNCAMUNCA. Oh! fie upon you, Sir, you make me blush. 5
TOM THUMB. It is the Virgin's Sign, and suits you well:
(m) I know not where, nor how, nor what I am,
(n) I'm so transported, I have lost my self.
HUNCAMUNCA. Forbid it, all ye Stars, for you're so small,
That were you lost, you'd find your self no more. 10
So the unhappy Sempstress once, they say,

(m) *Nor know I whether.*
What am I, who or where, Busiris.
I was I know not what, and am I know not how. Gloriana.

(n) To understand sufficiently the Beauty of this Passage, it will be necessary that we comprehend every Man to contain two Selfs. I shall not attempt to prove this from Philosophy, which the Poets make so plainly evident.

One runs away from the other;

Let me demand your Majesty, 5
Why fly you from your self? Duke of Guise.

In a 2*d*. One Self is a Guardian to the other;

Leave me the Care of me. Conquest of Granada.

Again, *My self am to my self less near.* Ibid.

In the same, the first Self is proud of the second; 10

I my self am proud of me. State of Innocence.

In a 3*d*. Distrustful of him;

Fain I would tell, but whisper it in mine Ear,
That none besides might hear, nay not my self. Earl of Essex.

In a 4*th*. Honours him; 15

I honour Rome,
But honour too my self. Sophonisba.

In a 5*th*. At Variance with him;

Leave me not thus at Variance with my self. Busiris.

Again, in a 6*th*. 20

I find my self divided from my self. Medea.

She seemed the sad Effigies of her self. Albion Queens.

Assist me, Zulema, *if thou would'st be*
The Friend thou seemest, assist me against me.

From all which it appears, that there are two Selfs; and therefore *Tom Thumb's* losing himself is no such Solecism as it hath been represented by Men, rather ambitious of Criticizing, than qualify'd to Criticize. 25

Her Needle in a Pottle, lost, of Hay;
In vain she look'd, and look'd, and made her Moan,
For ah, the Needle was for ever gone.

PARSON. Long may they live, and love, and propagate, 15
Till the whole Land be peopled with *Tom Thumbs*.
(p) So when the *Cheshire* Cheese a Maggot breeds,
Another and another still succeeds.
By thousands, and ten thousands they increase,
Till one continued Maggot fills the rotten Cheese. 20

SCENE X

NOODLE, *and then* GRIZZLE.

NOODLE. (q) Sure Nature means to break her solid Chain,
Or else unfix the World, and in a Rage,
To hurl it from its Axle-tree and Hinges;
All things are so confus'd, the King's in Love,
The Queen is drunk, the Princess married is. 5

GRIZZLE. Oh! *Noodle*, hast thou *Huncamunca* seen?

NOODLE. I've seen a Thousand Sights this day, where none
Are by the wonderful Bitch herself outdone,
The King, the Queen, and all the Court are Sights.

GRIZZLE. (r) D—n your Delay, you Trifler, are you drunk, ha? 10
I will not hear one Word but *Huncamunca*.

(p) Mr. *F* —— imagines this Parson to have been a *Welsh* one from his Simile.

(q) Our Author hath been plunder'd here according to Custom;

Great Nature break thy Chain *that links together,*
The Fabrick of the World and make a Chaos,
Like that within my Soul. Love Triumphant.

— Startle Nature, unfix the Globe, 5
And hurl it from its Axle-tree and Hinges. Albion Queens.

The tott'ring Earth seems sliding off its Props.

(r) *D——n your delay, ye Torturers proceed,*
I will not hear one Word but Almahide. Conq. of Granada.

NOODLE. By this time she is married to *Tom Thumb*.
GRIZZLE. [s] My *Huncamunca*.
NOODLE. Your *Huncamunca*.
Tom Thumb's Huncamunca, every Man's *Huncamunca*. 15
GRIZZLE. If this be true all Womankind are damn'd.
NOODLE. If it be not, may I be so my self.
GRIZZLE. See where she comes! I'll not believe a Word
Against that Face, upon whose [t] ample Brow,
Sits Innocence with Majesty Enthron'd. 20

GRIZZLE, HUNCAMUNCA.

GRIZZLE. Where has my *Huncamunca* been? See here
The Licence in my Hand!
HUNCAMUNCA. Alas! *Tom Thumb*.
GRIZZLE. Why dost thou mention him?
HUNCAMUNCA. Ah me! *Tom Thumb*. 25
GRIZZLE. What means my lovely *Huncamunca*?
HUNCAMUNCA. Hum!
GRIZZLE. Oh! Speak.
HUNCAMUNCA. Hum!
GRIZZLE. Ha! your every Word is Hum 30
[u] You force me still to answer you *Tom Thumb*.
Tom Thumb, I'm on the Rack, I'm in a Flame,
[x] *Tom Thumb, Tom Thumb, Tom Thumb*, you love the Name;
So pleasing is that Sound, that were you dumb
You still would find a Voice to cry *Tom Thumb*. 35
HUNCAMUNCA. Oh! Be not hasty to proclaim my Doom,
My ample Heart for more than one has Room,
A Maid like me, Heaven form'd at least for two,

(s) Mr. *Dryden* hath imitated this in *All for Love*.

(t) This Miltonick Stile abounds in the New *Sophonisba*.

— And on her ample Brow
Sat Majesty.

(u) *Your ev'ry Answer, still so ends in that,*
You force me still to answer you Morat. Aurengzebe.

(x) Morat, Morat, Morat, *you love the Name*. Aurengzebe.

(y)I married him, and now I'll marry you.
GRIZZLE. Ha! dost thou own thy Falshood to my Face? 40
Think'st thou that I will share thy Husband's place,
Since to that Office one cannot suffice,
And since you scorn to dine one single Dish on,
Go, get your Husband put into Commission,
Commissioners to discharge, (ye Gods) it fine is, 45
The duty of a Husband to your Highness;
Yet think not long, I will my Rival bear,
Or unreveng'd the slighted Willow wear;
The gloomy, brooding Tempest now confin'd,
Within the hollow Caverns of my Mind, 50
In dreadful Whirl, shall rowl along the Coasts,
Shall thin the Land of all the Men it boasts,
(z)And cram up ev'ry Chink of Hell with Ghosts.
*So have I seen, in some dark Winter's Day,
A sudden Storm rush down the Sky's High-Way, 55
Sweep thro' the Streets with terrible ding dong,

(y) Here is a Sentiment for the Virtuous *Huncamunca* (says Mr. *D——s*) and yet with the leave of this great Man, the Virtuous *Panthea* in *Cyrus*, hath an Heart every whit as Ample;

For two I must confess are Gods to me,
Which is my Abradatus *first, and thee.* Cyrus the Great. 5

Nor is the Lady in *Love Triumphant* more reserv'd, tho' not so intelligible;

— I am so divided,
That I grieve most for both, and love both most.

(z) A ridiculous Supposition to any one, who considers the great and extensive Largeness of Hell, says a Commentator: But not so to those who consider the great Expansion of immaterial Substance. Mr. *Banks* makes one Soul to be so expanded that Heaven could not contain it;

The Heavens are all too narrow for her Soul. Virtue Betray'd. 5

The *Persian Princess* hath a Passage not unlike the Author of this;

We will send such Shoals of murther'd Slaves,
Shall glut Hell's empty Regions.

This threatens to fill Hell even tho' it were empty; Lord *Grizzle* only to fill up the Chinks, supposing the rest already full. 10

* Mr. *Addison* is generally thought to have had this Simile in his Eye, when he wrote that beautiful one at the end of the third Act of his *Cato*.

Gush thro' the Spouts, and wash whole Crowds along.
The crowded Shops, the thronging Vermin skreen,
Together cram the Dirty and the Clean,
And not one Shoe-Boy in the Street is seen. 60

HUNCAMUNCA. Oh! fatal Rashness should his Fury slay,
My hapless Bridegroom on his Wedding Day;
I, who this Morn, of two chose which to wed,
May go again this Night alone to Bed;
(†)So have I seen some wild unsettled Fool, 65
Who had her Choice of this, and that Joint Stool;
To give the Preference to either, loath
And fondly coveting to sit on both:
While the two Stools her Sitting Part confound,
Between 'em both fall Squat upon the Ground. 70

THE END OF THE SECOND ACT.

---

† This beautiful Simile is founded on a Proverb, which does Honour to the *English* Language;

Between two Stools the Breech falls to the Ground.

I am not so pleased with any written Remains of the Ancients, as with those little Aphorisms, which verbal Tradition hath delivered down to us, under 5 the Title of Proverbs. It were to be wished that instead of filling their Pages with the fabulous Theology of the Pagans, our modern Poets would think it worth their while to enrich their Works with the Proverbial Sayings of their Ancestors. Mr. *Dryden* hath chronicl'd one in Heroick;

Two ifs scarce make one Possibility. Conquest of Granada. 10

My Lord *Bacon* is of Opinion, that whatever is known of Arts and Sciences might be proved to have lurked in the Proverbs of *Solomon*. I am of the same Opinion in relation to those abovemention'd: At least I am confident that a more perfect System of Ethicks, as well as Oeconomy, might be compiled out of them, than is at present extant, either in the Works of the 15 Antient Philosophers, or those more valuable, as more voluminous, ones of the modern Divines.

ACT III

SCENE I

SCENE, *King* Arthur's *Palace.*
[(a)] GHOST *solus.*

GHOST. Hail! ye black Horrors of Midnight's Midnoon!
Ye Fairies, Goblins, Bats and Screech-Owls, Hail!
And Oh! ye mortal Watchmen, whose hoarse Throats
Th' Immortal Ghosts dread Croakings counterfeit,
All Hail! — Ye dancing Fantoms, who by Day, 5
Are some condemn'd to fast, some feast in Fire;
Now play in Church-yards, skipping o'er the Graves,
To the [(b)] loud Musick of the silent Bell,
All Hail!

(a) Of all the Particulars in which the modern Stage falls short of the ancient, there is none so much to be lamented, as the great Scarcity of Ghosts in the latter. Whence this proceeds, I will not presume to determine. Some are of opinion, that the Moderns are unequal to that sublime Language which a Ghost ought to speak. One says ludicrously, That Ghosts are out of 5 Fashion; another, That they are properer for Comedy; forgetting, I suppose, that *Aristotle* hath told us, That a Ghost is the Soul of Tragedy; for so I render the Ψυχή ὁ μῦθος τῆς τραγωδίας which M. *Dacier*, amongst others, hath mistaken; I suppose mis-led, by not understanding the *Fabula* of the *Latins*, which signifies a *Ghost* as well as a *Fable.* 10

— *Te premet nox, fabulaeque Manes.* Hor.

Of all the Ghosts that have ever appeared on the Stage, a very learned and judicious foreign Critick, gives the Preference to this of our Author. These are his Words, speaking of this Tragedy;

— *Nec quidquam in illâ admirabilius quam Phasma quoddam horrendum,* 15 *quod omnibus aliis Spectris, quibuscum scatet Anglorum Tragaedia, longè (pace D —— isii V. Doctiss. dixerim) praetulerim.*

(b) We have already given Instances of this Figure.

SCENE II

KING, *and* GHOST.

KING. What Noise is this? — What Villain dares,
At this dread Hour, with Feet and Voice prophane,
Disturb our Royal Walls?
GHOST. One who defies
Thy empty Power to hurt him; (c) one who dares 5
Walk in thy Bed-Chamber.
KING. Presumptuous Slave!
Thou diest!
GHOST. Threaten others with that Word,
(d) I am a Ghost, and am already dead. 10
KING. Ye Stars! 'tis well; were thy last Hour to come,
This Moment had been it; (e) yet by thy Shrowd

(c) *Almanzor* reasons in the same manner;

— A Ghost I'll be,
And from a Ghost, you know, no Place is free.

Conq. of *Granada.*

(d) *The Man who writ this wretched Pun* (says Mr. *D.*) *would have picked your Pocket:* Which he proceeds to shew, not only bad in it self, but doubly so on so solemn an Occasion. And yet in that excellent Play of *Liberty Asserted,* we find something very much resembling a Pun in the Mouth of a Mistress, who is parting with the Lover she is fond of; 5

Ul. *Oh, mortal Woe! one Kiss, and then farewel.*
Irene. *The Gods have given to others to fare well.*
O miserably must Irene *fare.*

Agamemnon, in the *Victim,* is full as facetious on the most solemn Occasion, that of Sacrificing his Daughter; 10

Yes, Daughter, yes; you will assist the Priest;
Yes, you must offer up your — Vows for Greece.

(e) *I'll pull thee backwards by thy Shrowd to Light,*
Or else, I'll squeeze thee, like a Bladder, there,
And make thee groan thy self away to Air.

Conquest of *Granada.*

Snatch me, ye Gods, this Moment into Nothing.

Cyrus the Great.

I'll pull thee backward, squeeze thee to a Bladder,
'Till thou dost groan thy Nothingness away.

GHOST *retires.*

Thou fly'st! 'Tis well. 15
(f) I thought what was the Courage of a Ghost!
Yet, dare not, on thy Life — Why say I that,
Since Life thou hast not? — Dare not walk again,
Within these Walls, on pain of the *Red-Sea.*
For, if henceforth I ever find thee here, 20
As sure, sure as a Gun, I'll have thee laid —

GHOST. Were the *Red-Sea*, a Sea of *Holland's* Gin,
The Liquor (when alive) whose very Smell
I did detest, did loath — yet for the Sake
Of *Thomas Thumb*, I would be laid therein. 25

KING. Ha! said you?

GHOST. Yes, my Liege, I said *Tom Thumb*,
Whose Father's Ghost I am — once not unknown
To mighty *Arthur*. But, I see, 'tis true,
The dearest Friend, when dead, we all forget. 30

KING. 'Tis he, it is the honest Gaffer *Thumb.*
Oh! let me press thee in my eager Arms,
Thou best of Ghosts! Thou something more than Ghost!

GHOST. Would I were Something more, that we again
Might feel each other in the warm Embrace. 35
But now I have th' Advantage of my King,
(g) For I feel thee, whilst thou dost not feel me.

(f) *So, art thou gone? Thou canst no Conquest boast,*
I thought what was the Courage of a Ghost.

Conquest of *Granada.*

King *Arthur* seems to be as brave a Fellow as *Almanzor*, who says most heroically,

— *In spight of Ghosts, I'll on.* 5

(g) The Ghost of *Lausaria* in *Cyrus* is a plain Copy of this, and is therefore worth reading.

Ah, Cyrus!
Thou may'st as well grasp Water, or fleet Air,
As think of touching my immortal Shade. *Cyrus* the Great. 5

KING. But say, (h) thou dearest Air, Oh! say, what Dread,
Important Business sends thee back to Earth?
GHOST. Oh! then prepare to hear — which, but to hear, 40
Is full enough to send thy spirit hence.
Thy Subjects up in Arms, by *Grizzle* led,
Will, ere the rosy finger'd Morn shall ope
The Shutters of the Sky, before the Gate
Of this thy Royal Palace, swarming spread: 45
(i) So have I seen the Bees in Clusters swarm,
So have I seen the Stars in frosty Nights,
So have I seen the Sand in windy Days,
So have I seen the Ghosts on *Pluto's* Shore,
So have I seen the Flowers in Spring arise, 50
So have I seen the Leaves in *Autumn* fall,
So have I seen the Fruits in Summer smile,
So have I seen the Snow in Winter frown.
KING. D——n all thou'st seen! — Dost thou, beneath the Shape
Of Gaffer *Thumb*, come hither to abuse me, 55
With Similies to keep me on the Rack?
Hence — or by all the Torments of thy Hell,
(k) I'll run thee thro' the Body, tho' thou'st none.
GHOST. *Arthur*, beware; I must this Moment hence,
Not frighted by your Voice, but by the Cocks; 60
Arthur beware, beware, beware, beware!
Strive to avert thy yet impending Fate;
For if thou'rt kill'd To-day,
To-morrow all thy Care will come too late.

(h) *Thou better Part of heavenly Air.* Conquest of *Granada.*

(i) *A String of Similies* (says one) *proper to be hung up in the Cabinet of a Prince.*

(k) This Passage hath been understood several different Ways by the Commentators. For my Part, I find it difficult to understand it at all. Mr. *Dryden* says,

I have heard something how two Bodies meet,
But how two Souls join, I know not. 5

So that 'till the Body of a Spirit be better understood, it will be difficult to understand how it is possible to run him through it.

SCENE III

KING *solus*.

KING. Oh! stay, and leave me not uncertain thus!
And whilst thou tellest me what's like my Fate,
Oh, teach me how I may avert it too!
Curst be the Man who first a Simile made!
Curst, ev'ry Bard who writes! — So have I seen 5
Those whose Comparisons are just and true,
And those who liken things not like at all.
The Devil is happy, that the whole Creation
Can furnish out no Simile to his Fortune.

SCENE IV

KING, QUEEN.

QUEEN. What is the Cause, my *Arthur*, that you steal
Thus silently from *Dollallolla's* Breast?
Why dost thou leave me in the [l] Dark alone,
When well thou know'st I am afraid of Sprites?
KING. Oh *Dollallolla*! do not blame my Love; 5
I hop'd the Fumes of last Night's Punch had laid
Thy lovely Eye-lids fast. — But, Oh! I find
There is no Power in Drams, to quiet Wives;
Each Morn, as the returning Sun, they wake,
And shine upon their Husbands. 10
QUEEN. Think, Oh think!
What a Surprize it must be to the Sun,
Rising, to find the vanish'd World away.
What less can be the wretched Wife's Surprize,
When, stretching out her Arms to fold thee fast, 15
She folds her useless Bolster in her Arms.

(l) *Cydaria* is of the same fearful Temper with *Dollallolla*;
I never durst in Darkness be alone. Ind. Emp.

(m) Think, think on that — Oh! think, think well on that.
I do remember also to have read
(n) In *Dryden's Ovid's Metamorphosis*,
That *Jove* in Form inanimate did lie 20
With beauteous *Danae*; and trust me, Love,
(o) I fear'd the Bolster might have been a *Jove*.

KING. Come to my Arms, most virtuous of thy Sex;
Oh *Dollallolla*! were all Wives like thee,
So many Husbands never had worn Horns. 25
Should *Huncamunca* of thy Worth partake,
Tom Thumb indeed were blest. — Oh fatal Name!
For didst thou know one Quarter what I know,
Then would'st thou know — Alas! what thou would'st know!

QUEEN. What can I gather hence? Why dost thou speak 30
Like Men who carry *Raree-Shows* about,
Now you shall see, Gentlemen, what you shall see?
O tell me more, or thou hast told too much.

SCENE V

KING, QUEEN, NOODLE.

NOODLE. Long Life attend your Majesties serene,
Great *Arthur*, King, and *Dollallolla*, Queen!
Lord *Grizzle*, with a bold, rebellious Crowd,
Advances to the Palace, threat'ning loud,
Unless the Princess be deliver'd straight, 5
And the victorious *Thumb*, without his Pate,
They are resolv'd to batter down the Gate.

(m) *Think well of this, think that, think every way.* Sophonisba.

(n) These Quotations are more usual in the Comick, than in the Tragick Writers.

(o) *This Distress* (says Mr. *D*——) *I must allow to be extremely beautiful, and tends to heighten the virtuous Character of* Dollallolla, *who is so exceeding delicate, that she is in the highest Apprehension from the inanimate Embrace of a Bolster. An Example worthy of Imitation from all our Writers of Tragedy.*

SCENE VI

KING, QUEEN, HUNCAMUNCA, NOODLE.

KING. See where the Princess comes! Where is *Tom Thumb*?
HUNCAMUNCA. Oh! Sir, about an Hour and half ago
He sallied out to encounter with the Foe,
And swore, unless his Fate had him mis-led,
From *Grizzle's* Shoulders to cut off his Head, 5
And serve't up with your Chocolate in Bed.
KING. 'Tis well, I find one Devil told us both.
Come, *Dollallolla*, *Huncamunca*, come,
Within we'll wait for the victorious *Thumb*;
In Peace and Safety we secure may stay, 10
While to his Arm we trust the bloody Fray;
Tho' Men and Giants should conspire with Gods,
(p) He is alone equal to all these Odds.
QUEEN. He is indeed, a (q) Helmet to us all,

(p) *Credat Judaeus Apelles.*
Non ego — (Says Mr. *D.*) — *For, passing over the Absurdity of being equal to Odds, can we possibly suppose a little insignificant Fellow — I say again, a little insignificant Fellow able to vie with a Strength which all the* Sampsons *and* Hercules's *of Antiquity would be unable to encounter.* 5

I shall refer this incredulous Critick to Mr. *Dryden's* Defence of his *Almanzor*; and lest that should not satisfy him, I shall quote a few Lines from the Speech of a much braver Fellow than *Almanzor*, Mr. *Johnson's Achilles;*

Tho' Human Race rise in embattel'd Hosts,
To force her from my Arms — Oh! Son of Atreus! 10
By that immortal Pow'r, whose deathless Spirit
Informs this Earth, I will oppose them all. Victim.

(q) *I have heard of being supported by a Staff* (says Mr. *D.*) *but never of being supported by an Helmet.* I believe he never heard of Sailing with Wings, which he may read in no less a Poet than Mr. *Dryden*;

Unless we borrow Wings, and sail thro' Air.
Love Triumphant. 5

What will he say to a kneeling Valley?

— *I'll stand*
Like a safe Valley, that low bends the Knee,
To some aspiring Mountain. Injur'd Love.

While he supports, we need not fear to fall; 15
His Arm dispatches all things to our Wish,
And serves up every Foe's Head in a Dish.
Void is the Mistress of the House of Care,
While the good Cook presents the Bill of Fare;
Whether the Cod, that Northern King of Fish, 20
Or Duck, or Goose, or Pig, adorn the Dish.
No Fears the Number of her Guests afford,
But at her Hour she sees the Dinner on the Board.

SCENE VII

⟨SCENE⟩, *a Plain.*
Lord GRIZZLE, FOODLE, *and Rebels.*

GRIZZLE. Thus far our Arms with Victory are crown'd;
For tho' we have not fought, yet we have found
(r) No Enemy to fight withal.
FOODLE. Yet I,
Methinks, would willingly avoid this Day, 5
(s) This First of *April*, to engage our Foes.
GRIZZLE. This Day, of all the Days of th' Year, I'd choose,
For on this Day my Grandmother was born.
Gods! I will make *Tom Thumb* an *April* Fool;
(t) Will teach his Wit an Errand it ne'er knew, 10
And send it Post to the *Elysian* Shades.

I am asham'd of so ignorant a Carper, who doth not know that an Epithet 10
in Tragedy is very often no other than an Expletive. Do not we read in the
New *Sophonisba* of *grinding Chains, blue Plagues, white Occasions,* and *blue Serenity*? Nay, 'tis not the Adjective only, but sometimes half a Sentence
is put by way of Expletive, as, *Beauty pointed high with Spirit,* in the same
Play — and, *In the Lap of Blessing, to be most curst,* in the Revenge. 15

(r) A Victory like that of *Almanzor*.
Almanzor *is victorious without Fight.* Conq. of *Granada.*

(s) *Well have we chose an happy Day for Fight,*
For every Man in course of Time has found,
Some Days are lucky, some unfortunate. K. *Arthur.*

(t) We read of such another in *Lee;*
Teach his rude Wit a Flight she never made,
And send her Post to the Elysian *Shade.* Gloriana.

FOODLE. I'm glad to find our Army is so stout,
Nor does it move my Wonder less than Joy.
GRIZZLE. (u) What Friends we have, and how we came so strong,
I'll softly tell you as we march along. 15

SCENE VIII

Thunder and Lightning.
TOM THUMB, GLUMDALCA *cum suis.*

TOM THUMB. Oh, *Noodle*! hast thou seen a Day like this?
(x) The unborn Thunder rumbles o'er our Heads,
(y) As if the Gods meant to unhinge the World;
And Heaven and Earth in wild Confusion hurl;
Yet will I boldly tread the tott'ring Ball. 5
MERLIN. *Tom Thumb!*
TOM THUMB. What Voice is this I hear?
MERLIN. *Tom Thumb!*
TOM THUMB. Again it calls.
MERLIN. *Tom Thumb!* 10
GLUMDALCA. It calls again.
TOM THUMB. Appear, whoe'er thou art, I fear thee not.
MERLIN. Thou hast no Cause to fear, I am thy Friend,
Merlin by Name, a Conjuror by Trade,
And to my Art thou dost thy Being owe. 15
TOM THUMB. How!
MERLIN. Hear then the mystick Getting of *Tom Thumb.*
(z) *His Father was a Ploughman plain,*
His Mother milk'd the Cow;
And yet the way to get a Son, 20

(u) These Lines are copied *verbatim* in the *Indian Emperor.*

(x) *Unborn Thunder rolling in a Cloud.* Conq. of *Gran.*

(y) *Were Heaven and Earth in wild Confusion hurl'd,*
Should the rash Gods unhinge the rolling World,
Undaunted, would I tread the tott'ring Ball,
Crush'd, but unconquer'd, in the dreadful Fall.
Female Warrior.

(z) See the History of *Tom Thumb,* pag. 2.

This Couple knew not how.
Until such time the good old Man
To learned Merlin *goes,*
And there to him, in great Distress,
In secret manner shows; 25
How in his Heart he wish'd to have
A Child, in time to come,
To be his Heir, tho' it might be
No biger than his Thumb:
Of which old Merlin *was foretold,*
That he his Wish should have; 30
And so a Son of Stature small,
The Charmer to him gave.

Thou'st heard the past, look up and see the future.

TOM THUMB. [(a)]Lost in Amazement's Gulph, my Senses sink; 35
See there, *Glumdalca*, see another [(b)]Me!

GLUMDALCA. O Sight of Horror! see, you are devour'd
By the expanded Jaws of a red Cow.

MERLIN. Let not these Sights deter thy noble Mind,
[(c)]For lo! a Sight more glorious courts thy Eyes; 40
See from a far a Theatre arise;
There, Ages yet unborn, shall Tribute pay
To the Heroick Actions of this Day:
Then Buskin Tragedy at length shall choose
Thy Name the best Supporter of her Muse. 45

TOM THUMB. Enough, let every warlike Musick sound,
We fall contented, if we fall renown'd.

(a) *— Amazement swallows up my Sense,*
And in th' impetuous Whirl of circling Fate,
Drinks down my Reason. *Pers.* Princess.

(b) *— I have outfaced my self,*
What! am I two? Is there another Me? K. *Arthur.*

(c) The Character of *Merlin* is wonderful throughout, but most so in this Prophetick Part. We find several of these Prophecies in the Tragick Authors, who frequently take this Opportunity to pay a Compliment to their Country, and sometimes to their Prince. None but our Author (who seems to have detested the least Appearance of Flattery) would have past by such an Opportunity of being a Political Prophet. 5

SCENE IX

Lord GRIZZLE, FOODLE, *Rebels, on one Side.*
TOM THUMB, GLUMDALCA, *on the other.*

FOODLE. At length the Enemy advances nigh,
[d]I hear them with my Ear, and see them with my Eye.
GRIZZLE. Draw all your Swords, for Liberty we fight,
[e]And Liberty the Mustard is of Life.
TOM THUMB. Are you the Man whom Men fam'd *Grizzle* name? 5
GRIZZLE. [f]Are you the much more fam'd *Tom Thumb*?
TOM THUMB. The same.
GRIZZLE. Come on, our Worth upon our selves we'll prove,
For Liberty I fight.
TOM THUMB. And I for Love. 10

A bloody Engagement between the two Armies here, Drums beating, Trumpets sounding, Thunder and Lightning. — They fight off and on several times. Some fall. GRIZZLE *and* GLUMDALCA *remain.*

GLUMDALCA. Turn, Coward, turn, nor from a Woman fly.
GRIZZLE. Away — thou art too ignoble for my Arm.
GLUMDALCA. Have at thy Heart.

(d) *I saw the Villain,* Myron, *with these Eyes I saw him.*
Busiris.

In both which Places it is intimated, that it is sometimes possible to see with other Eyes than your own.

(e) *This Mustard* (says Mr. *D.*) *is enough to turn one's Stomach: I would be glad to know what Idea the Author had in his Head when he wrote it.* This will be, I believe, best explained by a Line of Mr. *Dennis*;

And gave him Liberty, the Salt of Life. Liberty asserted.

The Understanding that can digest the one, will not rise at the other. 5

(f) Han. *Are you the Chief, whom Men fam'd* Scipio *call?*
Scip. *Are you the much more famous* Hannibal? *Hannib.*

GRIZZLE. Nay then, I thrust at thine.
GLUMDALCA. You push too well, you've run me thro' the Guts, 15
And I am dead.
GRIZZLE. Then there's an End of One.
TOM THUMB. When thou art dead, then there's an End of Two,
[(g)] Villain.
GRIZZLE. *Tom Thumb!* 20
TOM THUMB. Rebel!
GRIZZLE. *Tom Thumb!*
TOM THUMB. Hell!
GRIZZLE. *Huncamunca!*
TOM THUMB. Thou hast it there. 25
GRIZZLE. Too sure I feel it.
TOM THUMB. To Hell then, like a Rebel as you are,
And give my Service to the Rebels there.
GRIZZLE. Triumph not, *Thumb*, nor think thou shalt enjoy
Thy *Huncamunca* undisturb'd, I'll send 30
[(h)] My Ghost to fetch her to the other World;
[(i)] It shall but bait at Heaven, and then return.

[(g)] Dr. *Young* seems to have copied this Engagement in his *Busiris:*

Myr. *Villain!*
Mem. Myron!
Myr. *Rebel!*
Mem. Myron! 5
Myr. *Hell!*
Mem. Mandane

[(h)] This last Speech of my Lord *Grizzle*, hath been of great Service to our Poets;

— *I'll hold it fast*
As Life, and when Life's gone, I'll hold this last;
And if thou tak'st it from me when I'm slain, 5
I'll send my Ghost, and fetch it back again.

Conquest of *Granada.*

[(i)] *My Soul should with such Speed obey,*
It should not bait at Heaven to stop its way.

Lee seems to have had this last in his Eye;

'Twas not my Purpose, Sir, to tarry there,
I would but go to Heaven to take the Air. Gloriana. 5

(k) But, ha! I feel Death rumbling in my Brains,
(l) Some kinder Spright knocks softly at my Soul,
And gently whispers it to haste away: 35
I come, I come, most willingly I come.
(m) So; when some City Wife, for Country Air,
To *Hampstead*, or to *Highgate* does repair;
Her, to make haste, Her Husband does implore,
And cries, My Dear, *the Coach is at the Door.* 40
With equal Wish, desirous to be gone,
She gets into the Coach, and then she cries — *Drive on!*

TOM THUMB. With those last Words (n) he vomited his Soul,
Which, (o) like whipt Cream, the Devil will swallow down.
Bear off the Body, and cut off the Head, 45
Which I will to the King in Triumph lug;
Rebellion's dead, and now I'll go to Breakfast.

SCENE X

KING, QUEEN, HUNCAMUNCA, *and Courtiers.*

KING. Open the Prisons, set the Wretched free,
And bid our Treasurer disburse six Pounds
To pay their Debts. — Let no one weep To-day.
Come, *Dollallolla*; (p) Curse that odious Name!

(k) *A rising* Vapour rumbling *in my Brains.* Cleomenes.

(l) *Some kind Spright knocks softly at my Soul,*
To tell me Fate's at Hand.

(m) Mr. *Dryden* seems to have had this Simile in his Eye, when he says,
My Soul is packing up, *and just on Wing.*
Conquest of *Granada.*

(n) *And in a purple Vomit pour'd his Soul.* Cleomenes.

(o) *The Devil swallows vulgar Souls*
Like whipp'd Cream. Sebastian.

(p) *How I could curse my Name of* Ptolemy!
It is so long, it asks an Hour to write it.
By Heav'n! I'll change it into Jove, *or* Mars,
Or any other civil Monosyllable,
That will not tire my Hand. Cleomenes. 5

It is so long, it asks an Hour to speak it. 5
By Heavens! I'll change it into *Doll*, or *Loll*,
Or any other civil Monosyllable
That will not tire my Tongue. — Come, sit thee down.
Here seated, let us view the Dancer's Sports;
Bid 'em advance. This is the Wedding-Day 10
Of Princess *Huncamunca* and *Tom Thumb*;
Tom Thumb! who wins two Victories [q] To-day,
And this way marches, bearing *Grizzle's* Head.

A Dance here.

NOODLE. Oh! monstrous, dreadful, terrible, Oh! Oh!
Deaf be my Ears, for ever blind my Eyes! 15
Dumb be my Tongue! Feet lame! All Senses lost!
[r] Howl Wolves, grunt Bears, hiss Snakes, shriek all ye Ghosts!
KING. What does the Blockhead mean?
NOODLE. I mean, my Liege
[s] Only to grace my Tale with decent Horror; 20
Whilst from my Garret, twice two Stories high,
I look'd abroad into the Streets below;
I saw *Tom Thumb* attended by the Mob,
Twice Twenty Shoe-Boys, twice two Dozen Links,
Chairmen and Porters, Hackney-Coachmen, Whores; 25
Aloft he bore the grizly Head of *Grizzle*;
When of a sudden thro' the Streets there came
A Cow, of larger than the usual Size,
And in a Moment — guess, Oh! guess the rest!
And in a Moment swallow'd up *Tom Thumb*. 30
KING. Shut up again the Prisons, bid my Treasurer

---

[q] Here is a visible Conjunction of two Days in one, by which our Author may have either intended an Emblem of a Wedding; or to insinuate, that Men in the Honey-Moon are apt to imagine Time shorter than it is. It brings into my Mind a Passage in the Comedy call'd the *Coffee-House Politician*;

We will celebrate this Day at my House To-morrow. 5

[r] These beautiful Phrases are all to be found in one single Speech of *King Arthur*, or *The British Worthy*.

[s] *I was but teaching him to grace his Tale*
With decent Horror. Cleomenes.

Not give three Farthings out — hang all the *Culprits*,
Guilty or not — no matter — Ravish Virgins,
Go bid the Schoolmasters whip all their Boys;
Let Lawyers, Parsons, and Physicians loose, 35
To rob, impose on, and to kill the World.

NOODLE. Her Majesty the Queen is in a Swoon.

QUEEN. Not so much in a Swoon, but I have still
Strength to reward the Messenger of ill News.

Kills NOODLE.

NOODLE. Oh! I am slain. 40

CLEORA. My Lover's kill'd, I will revenge him so.

Kills the QUEEN.

HUNCAMUNCA. My Mamma kill'd! vile Murtheress, beware.

Kills CLEORA.

DOODLE. This for an old Grudge, to thy Heart.

Kills HUNCAMUNCA.

MUSTACHA. And this
I drive to thine, Oh *Doodle*! for a new one. 45
— *Kills* DOODLE.

KING. Ha! Murtheress vile, take that

Kills MUSTACHA.

(t)And take thou this.

Kills himself, and falls.

(t) We may say with *Dryden*,

Death did at length so many Slain forget,
And left the Tale, and took them by the Great.

I know of no Tragedy which comes nearer to this charming and bloody Catastrophe, than *Cleomenes*, where the Curtain covers five principal 5
Characters dead on the Stage. These Lines too,

I ask no Questions then, of Who kill'd Who?
The Bodies tell the Story as they lie.

seem to have belonged more properly to this Scene of our Author. — Nor can I help imagining they were originally his. The Rival Ladies too seem 10
beholden to this Scene;

So when the Child whom Nurse from Danger guards,
Sends *Jack* for Mustard with a Pack of Cards;
Kings, Queens and Knaves throw one another down, 50
'Till the whole Pack lies scatter'd and o'erthrown;
So all our Pack upon the Floor is cast,
And all I boast is — that I fall the last.

Dies.

FINIS.

We're now a Chain of Lovers link'd in Death,
Julia *goes first,* Gonsalvo *hangs on her,*
And Angelina *hangs upon* Gonsalvo,
As I on Angelina. 15

No Scene, I believe, ever received greater Honours than this. It was applauded by several *Encores*, a Word very unusual in Tragedy — And it was very difficult for the Actors to escape without a second Slaughter. This I take to be a lively Assurance of that fierce Spirit of Liberty which remains among us, and which Mr. *Dryden* in his *Essay* on *Dramatick* 20 *Poetry* hath observed — *Whether Custom* (says he) *hath so insinuated it self into our Countrymen, or Nature hath so formed them to Fierceness, I know not, but they will scarcely suffer Combats, and other Objects of Horror, to be taken from them.* — And indeed I am for having them encouraged in this Martial Disposition: Nor do I believe our Victories over the *French* have been 25 owing to any thing more than to those bloody Spectacles daily exhibited in our Tragedies, of which the *French* Stage is so entirely clear.

TEXTUAL NOTES

TOM THUMB

SIGLA

TT^{u} = *Tom Thumb*, 1730 (unsigned) in Folger and Bodleian Libraries.
TT^{s} = *Tom Thumb*, 1730 (signed Scriblerus Secondus) in British Museum and Folger Library.
SECOND = *Tom Thumb*, 1730, The Second Edition (signed Scriblerus Secundus) in British Museum.
THIRD = *Tom Thumb*, 1730, The Third Edition (signed Scriblerus Secundus) in British Museum. When the act and scene reference of TT^{u} does not correspond to act and scene in TT^{s}, I have given the reference to TT^{s} first, followed by the act and scene reference to TT^{u}, set off in brackets.
In the use of the shorthand symbols $_{\wedge}$, ~ and + I have followed the practice of Professor Fredson Bowers (see his edition of *The Dramatic Works of Thomas Dekker*, vol. I, p. xvii) and of R. B. McKerrow (see *Prolegomena for the Oxford Shakespeare*, pp. 73–89).

PREFACE

Preface does not appear in TT^{u}.
39 fn. *Prefatical Language.*] THIRD; ~ ~, TT^{s}+.

PROLOGUE

Prologue does not appear in TT^{u}.

EPILOGUE

Epilogue does not appear in TT^{u}.

DRAMATIS PERSONAE

10 CLEORA, Mrs. *Smith.*] TT^{s}+; ~. TT^{u}.
11 MUSTACHA, Mrs. *Clark.*] TT^{s}+; ~. TT^{u}.
12 *Courtiers, Slaves, Bailiffs,* &c.] TT^{s}+; Slaves, *&c.* TT^{u}.
13 SCENE *The* . . . Arthur.] TT^{s}+; *omitted* TT^{u}.

I. III

17 Blossoms; like] THIRD; ~, ~ TT^{s}+.
59 S.D. *Exeunt all but* GRIZZLE.] TT^{u}; *omitted* TT^{s}+.

I. V.

14 on a Stile] TT^{s}+; on a Stall TT^{u}.

47 one of the two Dogs meets] TT^{s}+; the Dog contending meets TT^{u}.

II. I

This scene does not appear in TT^{u}.

II. II

This scene does not appear in TT^{u}

II. III

S.D. [II. I] *The Princess* Huncamunca's *Apartment*.] TT^{s}+; *omitted* TT^{u}.

1 [II. I. 1] Soul:] TT^{s}+; ~, TT^{u}.

II. VII

2 [II. V. 2]$_{\wedge}$ for even now] TT^{s}+;— ~ ~ ~ TT^{u}.

6 [II. V. 6] Ye Blazing Stars] TT^{s}+; Ye Charming Stars TT^{u}.

II. VIII

8 [II. VI. 8] dress'd up Monkey] TT^{s}+; dress'd Monkey TT^{u}.

9 [II. VI. 9] Son-in-Law!] TT^{s}+; ~, TT^{u}.

22–23 [II. VI. 22–23] Sempstress, once, they say,/ Her Needle in a Pottle, lost, of Hay.] TT^{s}+; Sempstress lost, they say, / Her Needle in a Bottle full of Hay, TT^{u}.

26 [II. VI] The King's final speech does not appear in TT^{u}.

II. IX

10 [II. VII. 10] Doctor] TT^{s}+; So Doctor TT^{u}.

II. X

5 [II. VIII. 5] Be he]; Be He THIRD, TT^{u}; But he TT^{s}+.

II. XI

1 [II. IX. 1] Wretched] TT^{s}+; wretched TT^{u}.

3 [II. IX. 3] Debts. —Let] TT^{s}+; ~$_{\wedge}$—let TT^{u}.

5 [II. IX. 5] Sport;] TT^{s}+; ~, TT^{u}.

6 [II. IX. 6] advance.—This] TT^{s}+; ~$_{\wedge}$—this TT^{u}.

II. *The Last*

S.D. *Last.*] TT^{s}+; *last*$_{\wedge}$ TT^{u}.

1 Oh$_{\wedge}$ monstrous! dreadful! terrible!] TT^{s}+; ~! Monstrous! Dreadful! Terrible! TT^{u}.

11 A Cow, of] TT^{s}+; ~ ~$_{\wedge}$ ~ TT^{u}.

12 Moment] TT^{s}+; moment TT^{u}.

13 Moment] TT^{s}+; moment TT^{u}.

19 Treasurer] THIRD, TT^{u}; Tresaurer TT^{s}+.

21 matter.—Ravish] TT^{s}+; ~$_{\wedge}$ — ravish TT^{u}.

25 *Tom*] TT^{s}+; *Thom* TT^{u}.

28 I'll kill thy Ghost.] TT^{s}, SECOND; I'll kill the Ghost. TT^{u}; I'll thy Ghost. THIRD.

29 Deed!—I] TT^{s}+; — TT^{u}~~$_{\wedge}$.

THE TRAGEDY OF TRAGEDIES

SIGLA

N.Y.P. = New York Public Library copy.
HARVARD = Harvard Library copy.
B.M. = British Museum copies.
U. of P. = University of Pennsylvania Library copy.
HILLHOUSE = unlocated "impression" cited in J. T. Hillhouse edition of *The Tragedy of Tragedies.*
3RD = 1737 edition.
1730 ED. = 1730 first edition of *Tom Thumb* (signed Scriblerus Secundus).
References to footnotes in Fielding's text may be exemplified thus: I. III. 27*z*7 = seventh line of footnote *z* annexed to line 27 of Act I, scene III.

PREFACE

1–2 concerning] HILLHOUSE, 3RD; concernining N.Y.P.+.
83 Features? The] 3RD; ~. ~ N.Y.P.+.
93 us, in] 3RD; ~. In N.Y.P.+.
99–100 is the *Action*] 3rd; is the the *Action* N.Y.P.+.
101 *Tom*] 3RD; *Tomb* N.Y.P.+.

I. I

18*e*12 understand] U. of P., HILLHOUSE, 3RD; undestand N.Y.P.+.

I. II

1*l*1 with King] 3RD; wirh King N.Y.P.+.

I. III

3 me?] 3RD; ~. N.Y.P.+.
17 me:] 3RD; ~. N.Y.P.+.
27*z*7 as a] U. of P., HILLHOUSE, 3RD; asa N.Y.P.+.
45 choose] U. of P., HILLHOUSE, 3RD; chose N.Y.P.+.
65*f*1 use.] 3RD; ~‸ N.Y.P.+.
66*g*5 *listening*] *listning* N.Y.P.+.
89*k*2 *Fate?*] ~, N.Y.P.+.
89*k*3 *Dog?*] 3RD; ~. N.Y.P.+.
90 dost? Me] 3RD; ~. ~ N.Y.P.+.
94*m*3 Queens.] 3RD; Queen‸ N.Y.P. +.

I. IV

8 low.] 3RD; ~‸ N.Y.P.+.

I. V

31 We will; (*u*)] HILLHOUSE; ~ ~‸ ~ N.Y.P.+.
52–53 art‸ / A setting Dog, be] 3RD, 1730 ED.; ~, / ~ ~ ~‸ ~ N.Y.P.+.

II. I

S.D. SCENE, *The*] SCENE$_\wedge$ ~ N.Y.P. +.

II. II

23*d*1–2 Mr. D——s. The] 3RD; ~ ~$_\wedge$ ~ N.Y.P.+.
38*e*6 *Fray's*] HILLHOUSE, 3RD; *Frays* N.Y.P.+.

II. IV

S.D. KING, HUNCAMUNCA] *King*, Huncamunca 3RD; ~$_\wedge$ ~ N.Y.P.+.
11*k*6 Banks'] Banks'*s* N.Y.P.+.

II. V

41*r*5 Queens.] 3RD; Queen$_\wedge$ N.Y.P. +.

II. VI

4 made$_\wedge$] 3RD; ~. N.Y.P.+.
5*u*6 State of Innocence.] ~ ~ Innocency$_\wedge$ N.Y.P.+.
5*u*19 Flint;] 3RD; ~. N.Y.P.+.

II. VII

13 (zz) The] (*z*) The N.Y.P.+.
13*z*1 (zz). A] (z) A N.Y.P.+.
30 does in his Fingers] 3RD; does in in his Fingers N.Y.P.+.

II. VIII

S.D. KING, GLUMDALCA.] King$_\wedge$ Glumdalca. N.Y.P.+.
2*e*1 Rags;] 3RD; ~. N.Y.P.+.
10*h*1–2 (*h*) —*I am a Multitude, | Of walking Griefs.*]—*I am a Multitude.* | (*h*) *Of walking Griefs.* N.Y.P.+.
20 King. (*l*) Oh!] King. Oh! N.Y.P. +.

II. IX

8*n*5 *Majesty*,] 3RD; ~? N.Y.P.+.
8*n*6 *self*?] 3RD; ~. N.Y.P.+.
8*n*14 Essex.] 3RD; ~$_\wedge$ N.Y.P.+.
8*n*22 Albion Queens.] Banks N.Y.P. +.
8*n*24 *against me.*] ~ ~. Albion Queens. N.Y.P.+.

II. X.

25 Ah$_\wedge$ me! *Tom*] 3RD; ~! ~$_\wedge$ ~ N.Y.P.+.
39*y*6 *Triumphant*$_\wedge$ more] 3RD; ~; ~ N.Y.P.+.
50 Mind,] 3RD; ~. N.Y.P.+.

III. I

S.D. SCENE, *King*] 3RD; ~$_\wedge$ ~ N.Y.P. +.
S.D.*a*8 μῦθος γῆς] μῦθθ ~ N.Y.P. +.

III. II

8 Thou diest!] ~ ~: N.Y.P.+.
10*d*7 *fare well.*] 3RD; *farewel.* N.Y.P. +.
10*d*8 *fare*] 3RD; *fair* N.Y.P.+.
58 (*k*) I'll] (*l*) I'll N.Y.P.+.

III. VI

13*p*1 *Apelles*] 3RD; *Appelles* N.Y.P. +
14*q*15 *curst*, in] ~. In N.Y.P.+.

III. IX

34 Soul,] 3RD; ~. N.Y.P.+.

III. X

8 down.] 3RD; ~, N.Y.P.+.
12 *Thumb!*] 3RD; *Thum!* N.Y.P.+.
15 blind$_\wedge$ my] 3RD, 1730 ED.; ~, ~ N.Y.P.+.

COMMENTARIES

TOM THUMB

PREFACE

7 Longinus] Samuel H. Monk makes clear in his book *The Sublime* (Ann Arbor, 1960) that on the basis of the pseudo-Longinian treatise, *Peri Hupsous* (known as Longinus, *On the Sublime*), Longinus was the chief authority on aesthetics in the eighteenth century, as Aristotle was on tragedy and drama in general.

7 *Scriblerus*] Pope used this pseudonym for his *Peri Bathos: or, The Art of Sinking in Poetry* (1728). In this version, Fielding only begins to see the potential of Scriblerus. In *The Tragedy of Tragedies*, Scriblerus is shifted from author to editor, giving Fielding an entire new range of burlesque.

8–9 *Hurlothrumbo*] a wild farce produced at the Little Haymarket Theatre in 1729 and written by Samuel Johnson, not Dr. Samuel Johnson but a dancing master of Cheshire.

11 *Charon* in *Lucian*] See *Dialogues of the Dead*, x. Like satirists from Marston to Roy Campbell, Fielding cites a classical satirist (Lucian was a second-century Greek satirist.) whose reputation as "blasphemer or slanderer" had been established, thereby linking this new satire with the satiric tradition.

13 Mr. *Lock*] See John Locke's *An Essay Concerning Human Understanding*, Bk. III, Ch. ii ff. "Of the Signification of Words". Perhaps because of his vogue, Locke was both Titan and butt for several eighteenth-century satirists, among them Sterne, Prior, and Fielding.

16–17 *Paraphonalia*] A *faux pas* by Colley Cibber in the "Address to the Reader" prefacing *The Provok'd Husband* (1728) in which he said that the actress Mrs Oldfield's costuming for this play "seem'd in all Respects, the *Paraphonalia* of a Woman of Quality". Fielding is playing with the etymology of the word and with Cibber's lack of even the most rudimentary grammar-school classical training.

20–1 *when the People . . . Ancestors*] a direct quotation from Cibber's "Address to the Reader."

25 *Cicero* observes] See Cicero, *Epistolae ad Atticorum*, VII. 13.

28 *quasi Plaface . . .*] The point of all this comic etymology is another thrust at actor, playwright, dandy, theatre manager, and aspiring poet laureat, Colley Cibber.

28–9 *A Plato*] from Plato.

35 This Preface then was writ . . .] the same pose that Swift assumes in his prefatory material to *The Tale of a Tub* (1710).

44 the first Scene of *OEdipus*] See first act stage direction to Dryden and Lee's *Oedipus* (London, 1679): "The Curtain rises to a plaintive tune, representing the present con-

dition of Thebes; Dead Bodies appear at a distance in the Streets; Some faintly go over the Stage, others drop."

49 *cum multis aliis*] with many others.

56 *Grubstreet*] The name of a street near Moorfields in London "much inhabited by writers of small histories, dictionaries, and temporary poems" according to Dr Samuel Johnson, generally a term of derogation for hack writers in the eighteenth century.

60 *vulgo*] commonly.

62 such are *Tom Tram*, *Hickathrift*, &c.] This ironic recommendation of folk heroes and the productions of contemporary hacks here and in the Prologue is Fielding's answer to attacks on the classics. Both Addison and Steele had recommended abandoning some of ancient mythology and lore in favour of native ballad material or of principles more in keeping with a Christian nation. The novelist Richardson would do the same later. Fielding, although no pedant like those he attacks in *The Tragedy of Tragedies*, was a careful student of classical literature and not interested in "folk" material, except ironically or as material for puppet shows. Both "Tom Tram" and "Hickathrift" were actual heroes of eighteenth-century penny-books (*A Pleasant and Delightful History of Thomas Hickathrift* and *The Mad Pranks of Tom Tram*). See John Ashton, *Chap-Books of the Eighteenth Century* (London, 1882). Hickathrift was a folk giant, six feet high and three feet thick at the age of ten.

79 my hearty Thanks to the Musick] These concluding paragraphs in praise of the actors and musicians are a general parody of Colley Cibber's "To The Reader" in his *The Provok'd Husband* (London, 1728).

84–5 *Seria cum . . . Causa es*—] "That I prefer to write on amusing topics, although I could write on serious ones, is your fault." Martial, *Epigrams*, v. 16.1.

PROLOGUE

By no Friend of the Author's] Swift had already parodied the eighteenth-century custom of having prologue and epilogue added by "friends of the author" in his *Tale of a Tub.* Fielding simply reverses the joke. Both make it clear that the "friends" were often the author himself.

8 Lee] Nathaniel Lee (1649–1692), playwright and collaborator with Dryden. He wrote eleven sorrowful tragedies.

EPILOGUE

1 Tom Thumb, *twice dead, is a third Time Reviv'd*] The character Tom Thumb is killed twice in the play; and the play, after its original run, "died" at the Little Haymarket Theatre at the end of the season in July, was revived in September at the Great Booth at the Southwark Fair, and then again revived for the new season at the Little Haymarket in October.

23 *But, for the Ladies*] This appeal to the ladies in the audience for support, often ironic and usually full of bawdy implication, had become a convention since the Restoration.

I. I

19 a Lump of Gristle] All of these references to Arthur and Merlin and to Thumb's bonelessness can

be found in the chap-book ballad of Tom Thumb. See Ashton, *Chap-Books*.

I. II

5 *Mother Demdike*] Elizabeth Southerns, the most important of a group of witches whose trial was held in Lancashire in 1612. This famous witch trial, at which ten were condemned to death, passed into folklore and even supplied material for literature. Thomas Shadwell based his *The Lancashire Witches* (London, 1681) on it. See W. Notestein, *A History of Witchcraft in England from 1558 to 1718* (New York, 1965), pp. 121–8.

I. III

6 Thy Modesty's a Candle to thy Merit] a comic expansion of the English proverb "to hold a candle to" (to surpass), a variant not recorded in the standard dictionaries of proverbs.

38 *Scipio*] Publius Cornelius Scipio Africanus, the great Roman general who defeated Hannibal in a decisive battle near Zama and who was principally responsible for the rolling back of the Carthaginian empire.

I. V

13–15 When in a Pudding . . . Was drop'd] one of the trials of Tom Thumb in the first part of the chap-book ballad "The Famous History of Tom Thumb".

26 smiling Dolphins] For the tale of the boy and the playful dolphins of Hippo see Pliny, the Younger, *Epistles*, 9.33. Edward Young had made reference to it in his "Naval Lyrick" put out only a few weeks before this play, and Fielding is ironically playing with Young's ability to make Pliny into "poetry".

34 Fox-hunters] F. Homes Dudden thinks this allusion to Walpole's favourite pastime would have linked Thumb and Sir Robert Walpole for Fielding's audience.

I. VI

13 *Tothill-Bridewell's*] Bridewell was simply a synonym for prison. The Gate House prison stood at the Western end of Tothill Street. In the early eighteenth century it was used mostly for debtors and prostitutes. A description of the imprisonment, punishment, and freeing of a prostitute (wench) follows. See Hogarth's *The Harlot's Progress*.

II. I

2–4 cudgell'd oft . . . hath been try'd] a list of trials visited on bailiffs by London crowds: they were beaten with clubs, thrown in blankets, held under public water-pumps, and thrown into horse-troughs. See Thomas Shadwell's *The Squire of Alsatea* (London, 1688) for a similar description of the bailiffs' trials. Fielding, when he became "first" magistrate for Westminster, was chiefly responsible tor creating a more efficient and honest police force (the Bow-Street runners) presumably bringing such treatment of officers of the law to an end.

7 Prize-fighter] Bare fist prize-fighting was coming into vogue about this time to compete with sports like bear and bull baiting, and cock-fighting. See A. S. Turberville, *English Men and Manners in the 18th Century* (Oxford, 1926).

II. II

36 dismal Shades] the underworld, the abode of the dead in classical mythology.

II. III

1 Give me some Musick] Song and dance were very much a part of theatre in the Restoration and eighteenth century. In fact, operas are often difficult to distinguish from the more ordinary dramatic tragedies. Dryden turned Milton's *Paradise Lost* into an opera called *The State of Innocence*. By the early part of the eighteenth century most major writers were appalled at the effect the opera was having on the theatre, and men as diverse as Pope, Richard Steele, and John Dennis feared that it would ultimately destroy legitimate drama. So, when Fielding ridiculed these mixed forms in this burlesque, he was in good company. The late seventeenth and early eighteenth-century dominance of the opera and musical entertainments did have a lasting effect on English drama, bringing to it an interest in elaborate staging that has become a part of theatrical convention.

13 mighty *Bantam*] a reference to Fielding's earlier burlesque called *The Author's Farce* (London, 1730), in which the poet Luckless is discovered to be Henry I, King of *Bantam*, on the death of his father Francis IV.

14 King of *Brentford*] This may be an allusion to Walpole's control of the elections in 1727. Brentford was election town for the Knights of the Shire of Middlesex county. This is also an allusion to *The Author's Farce*. In the last act, Harriet, Luckless' landlady's daughter, is discovered to be Harrietta, Princess of Old Brentford. This fortunate last act discovery allows Fielding to ridicule such fortunate accidents and to allude to Buckingham's *The Rehearsal* (London, 1671), an earlier burlesque of dramatic bombast. In it there are two Kings of Brentford.

19 his Horns] the conventional reference to the horns of a cuckold.

II. IV

15 yellow Blood of slaughter'd Giants] Yellow is the colour traditionally associated with witches, devils and giants in Demonology. See M. D. Conway, *Demonology and Devil-Lore* (New York, 1879).

II. V

12 by my Stars] Swearing by the stars was an old habit that grew out of the medieval belief that stars literally controlled man's destiny.

II. VI

4 *Paracelsus*] Swiss physician, alchemist (chemist), and natural philosopher (1490–1541). This believer in chemical remedies for diseases opposed Galenian and Hippocratic medicine.

5 *Hippocrates*] famous ancient Greek physician born about 460 B.C. His medical theory, founded on careful observation of symptoms, consisted chiefly of diet control and herbous remedies. He also expounded the theory of bodily humours.

5 *Galen*] celebrated medical writer who lived in the 2nd century A.D. His theory of medicine founded on the Hippocratic humours treated the

rampant humour with its opposite drug (*e.g.* a moist humour with a dry drug).

7–19 I bled him . . .] The remedies listed are those in use in the eighteenth century, and are essentially those of Hippocrates and Galen. Letting blood, plastering (Blister, Glister and *trahifick* Plaister) to draw out poison, and the various purges (*Cathartícks*, *Emeticks*, and *Diureticks*) were to relieve the excess of one or the other of the humours.

15–16 I would immediately have cut off his Arm] the second Physician, with his interest in Anatomy and surgery, is a follower of Galen, as the first Physician with his external and natural internal remedies, is a follower of Hippocrates.

II. VIII

5 Monkey] Monkeys and lap dogs were the common house pets of fashionable women in the eighteenth century.

11 the Temple] The Middle and Inner Temple, two of the four Inns of Court, situated by the Thames on the south side of Fleet Street, were the home of barristers and young lawyers. Here a quick legal marriage could be performed. Not until the Marriage Act of the Pelham administration in the 1750s was there any attempt to regulate marriages. Although a stamped marriage licence was required by law, even that was not essential. All that was needed was the consent of the couple, whether drunk or sober, and a willing clergyman.

22–5 the unhappy Sempstress . . .] One more English proverb is worked in here: "to seek a needle in a [bottle, pottle, bundle] of hay." The reference to a sempstress is a variant not recorded in the standard dictionaries of proverbs.

II. IX

S.D. *Manent*] They stay.

II. *The Last*

13 in a Moment swallow'd up *Tom Thumb*] The Tom Thumb of the ballad was swallowed and excreted by a cow, a Miller, a fish, etc.

S.D. *Kills the Ghost*] The ghost of Tom Thumb makes an appearance in part three of the ballad too.

38 *Jack* for Mustard] Jack-a-Mustard is a card game joke in which the cards are sprayed about and the butt must pick them up.

THE TRAGEDY OF TRAGEDIES

Comments on the material contained in *Tom Thumb* will not be repeated in these notes on *The Tragedy of Tragedies*.

PREFACE

4 Mr. *P*——] Mr Pope.

5 Mr. *F*——] Mr Fielding.

9–10 *Egregium & maximi . . . anteponendum*] a distinguished work of great value, to be rated as by far the best ancient or modern tragedy.

10–11 Dr. *B*——] Dr Richard Bentley (1662–1742), a great eighteenth-century classical scholar with whom both Pope and Swift had already had literary quarrels. Swift's *Battle of the Books* is part of the controversy which raged at the time between defenders of ancient and modern learning. Bentley was the chief defender of modern learning, and Sir William Temple (Swift's patron and employer) was one of the defenders of timeless ancient knowledge.

11–13 *Citiùs Maevii . . . dubitârim*] I should sooner have believed that Maevius wrote the *Aeneid* than that this tragedy, whose authorship I should have had no hesitation in ascribing to Seneca himself, were the work of that Scriblerus fellow. *cf.* Horace, *Epodes*, 10.2.

13 Professor *Burman*] Pieter Burmann (1688–1741), the Dutch classicist with whom Fielding studied while at Leyden in 1728. Burmann edited most of the Latin authors; his editions were thorough and pedantic.

14 *Heroum . . . Principem*] of all tragic heroes easily the foremost.

21 Mr. *D*——] Mr John Dennis (1657–1734). All of the most bad-tempered assertions in the footnotes will be found to be attributed to this irascible eighteenth-century critic. He, of course, did not make this assertion; but his *The Grounds of Criticism in Poetry* (1704), a dissertation on English literature designed to bring back to poetry, and particularly to dramatic poetry, "all its Greatness, and . . . its Innocence," is full of just this kind of assertion. Actually, it is one of the earliest English dissertations on the Sublime (see Monk, *The Sublime*, pp. 51–4). *The Critical Works of John Dennis*, ed. E. N. Hooker (Baltimore, 1939), I, p. 328. Scriblerus quarrels with Dennis throughout the footnotes, often "quoting' snatches that might be found anywhere or nowhere in Dennis.

27 piratical Copy] The pose here is that *Tom Thumb. a Tragedy*, published 24 Apr. 1730 and then extensively revised by Fielding to be acted and published in March of 1731, was a pirated and inaccurate copy of this play. A second edition of *Tom Thumb*, with an added prologue, epilogue, and preface, had even come out under Scriblerus' name in 1730.

51 *Clariss. Bentleium*] Richard Bentley.

56–57 written by *Shakespear*] See Pope's *Epistle to Arbuthnot*. The Shakespeare idolatry had already copy of this play. A second editions of Shakespeare in the eighteenth century. Both Pope and Samuel Johnson were among his eighteenth century editors.

63 *Tom Thumb*, was written in the Reign of Queen *Elizabeth*] This learned disquisition on dating is important to the transparent hoax that Fielding is creating. With careful pedantry, his scholar, Scriblerus, dates the play early enough so that works from 1639 to a pindaric ode only a few days old could borrow from *The Tragedy of Tragedies*. Actually, Fielding parodied "serious" authors from John Fletcher to Edward Young.

66–7 the *History of Tom Thumb*, . . . *London-Bridge*] a chap-book ballad probably published by Edward Midwinter who used this sign after 1721. See G. J. Gray's "The Booksellers of London Bridge and their Dwellings", in *Notes and Queries*, VI. 7 (1883), p. 462.

74 Mr. *M*——*r*] Midwinter.

75 Mr. *C*——*l*] probably the notori-

ous publisher Edmund Curll, attacked by Pope in *The Dunciad.*

76–77 the little Care . . . History] Fielding uses his ballad material for his own purposes, often political.

80–91 Nay, do we not . . . Ancients.] Fielding has Scriblerus point out the inconsistencies in the imaginative use to which history had been put by earlier playwrights: Jean Mairet, *Sophonisbe* (Paris, 1634); Nathaniel Lee, *Sophonisba* (London, 1676); Pierre Corneille, *Sophonisbe* (Paris, 1663); James Thomson, *The Tragedy of Sophonisba* (London, 1730); François Voltaire, *Brutus* (Paris, 1730); Thomas Otway, *The History and Fall of Caius Marius* (London, 1680). This may all be a parody of Corneille's preface "to the reader" attached to his *Sophonisbe.*

90 *Minerva*] goddess of intelligence, meditation and inventiveness.

91 *Venus*] goddess of the Spring, usually identified with the Greek love-goddess, Aphrodite.

93 I shall treat separately of . . .] Fielding demonstrates here that the most insignificant farce is a great tragedy simply by applying the standard eighteenth-century critical approach of pre-established rules and preconceived critical notions. Perhaps John Dennis represents this approach at its best and Thomas Rymer at its worst. Dryden, Pope and Fielding all attack these critics who insist on a kind of critical formalism that they had taken over from the French. For a similar critical approach, skillfully done, see Addison's essay on the ballad "Chevy-Chase" in *The Spectator*, No. 70, or his essays on Milton, *The Spectator*, Nos. 267, 273, 279, 285.

96–9 "One, regular, . . . Emotion."] a direct quotation from the Preface to Thomson's *Sophonisba.*

115 Mr. *D*——] Dennis.

121 Serjeant *Kite*] a character in George Farquhar's, *The Recruiting Officer* (London, 1706). In the opening speech of the play, Kite, in order to attract recruits says, "and he that has the good Fortune to be born six Foot high, was born to be a Great Man".

142 Image of two inns] For this image see the first paragraph of Dryden's *Of Heroique Playes, An Essay*" attached to *The Conquest of Granada* (London, 1672). Dryden is defending the use of thoughts, images, and actions "rais'd above the ordinary life".

146–7 *Telephus & . . . Verba*] Both Telephus and Peleus, when poor and in exile, abandoned grandiloquent words six feet long. Horace, *Epistola ad Pisones,* III. 96–7. Scriblerus grossly misinterprets Horace here. Horace used Telephus and Peleus as examples of execrable poets.

155 *dolere Sermone pedestri*] to grieve in ordinary speech. Horace, *Epistola ad Pisones,* III. 95.

160–2 *Quid est . . . Scientiâ*] Fielding translates this in the next lines, before the semi-colon.

166 *Omne genus . . . vincit*] In the matter of solemnity, tragedy outdoes all other kinds of writing. Ovid, *Tristium,* Liber II. 381.

167 *Bathos*] Everything that follows is an extrapolation on Pope's *Art of Sinking in Poetry* (1727), a mock treatise by Martinus Scriblerus, which elaborately defends the art of Bathos, or the Profound. Pope simply establishes the Profound as the other extreme from

Longinus' Sublime. Everything in between ("as Corn, Flowers, Fruits, Animals, and Things for the meer Use of Man, are of mean price, and so common as not to be greatly esteem'd by the Curious") he ironically dismisses. *The Art of Sinking in Poetry*, ed. E. L. Steeves, pp. 16–17. New York (Columbia U.P.) 1952.

187 *Earl of Essex*] John Banks, *The Unhappy Favourite: Or The Earl of Essex* (London, 1682).

192–3 *Quae non . . . legerim*] Things which I do not despise, because I have never read them. Cicero, *Tusculan Disputations*, II. 7.

I. I

1*a*1 Corneille recommends] See Corneille, *Oeuvres*, "Discours Des Trois Unitès" (Paris, 1862), p. 111.

1*a*6 *Cato*] Joseph Addison, *Cato* (London, 1713), I. I, (the opening speech, delivered by Portius).

1*a*6 *Mariamne*] Elijah Fenton, *Mariamne* (London, 1723), I. I, (the opening speech, delivered by Pheroras).

1*a*6 *Tamerlane*] Nicholas Rowe, *Tamerlane* (London, 1702), I. I, (the opening speech, delivered by Prince Tanais).

1*a*13 Caes. Borg.] Nathaniel Lee, *Caesar Borgia; Son of Pope Alexander the Sixth* (London, 1680), I. III (p. 11). Most of Fielding's footnoted lines were isolated by J. T. Hillhouse. Each has been checked, and a page reference given to the first edition.

1*a*18 *Like* Sophonisba] Thomson, *Sophonisba*, V. I, (p. 46).

1*a*26 *To Peep*, &c] Lewis Theobald, *The Persian Princess. Or, The Royal Villain* (London, 1715), IV. II, (p. 42).

7*b*3 State of Innocence] John Dryden, *The State of Innocence, and Fall of Man* (London, 1677), I. I, (p. 5).

7*b*4 Don Sebastian] John Dryden, *Don Sebastian, King of Portugal* (London, 1690), II. I, (p. 37).

7*b*5 Sophonisba] Thomson, *Sophonisba*, V. IV, (p. 54).

7*b*6 Revenge] Edward Young, *The Revenge* (London, 1721), IV. I, (p. 46).

8*c*1 Dr. *B——y*] Dr Bentley.

8*c*1 Mr. *D——s*] Mr Dennis.

8*c*2 Mr. *T——d*] Mr Theobald. Theobald had become one of the pedantic enemies of the Scriblerus Club by correcting Pope's edition of Shakespeare and then producing his own.

10*d*1 Mr. *S——n*] as Hillhouse suggests, probably Nathanael Salmon (1675–1742), a historian of Roman culture in Great Britain and a nonjuror who resigned his charge as curate at Westmill, Hertfordshire in 1702 rather than take an oath of allegiance to Queen Anne, although he had earlier taken an oath to William III. This reference to Salmon may indicate that Fielding was imitating Dr Wm. Wagstaffe's *A Comment upon the History of Tom Thumb* (1711) as well as Swift and Pope. Salmon had been satirised by Wagstaffe in footnote comments on the chap-book hero, Tom Thumb. Wagstaffe's *Comment* was also a satiric barb aimed at Addison's defence of "Chevy-Chase".

10*d*4 *Royal Villain*] See Theobald, *The Persian Princess*, IV. II, (p. 45). The "Giant *Greatness*" is not a giant at all but another bad metaphor by Theobald.

10*d*5–6 *Petrus Burmanus*] Pieter Burmann.

10*d*8 *Centaurs* slain by that Heroe] Hercules, worshipped as a God by the Greeks, once encountered the horse-men, Centaurs, when he visited the Centaur Pholus. Hercules beat off the attacking Centaurs. See Ovid's, *Metamorphoses*, Bk. XII.

10*d*9 *Hermes Trismegistus*] an awkward translation of the Egyptian "Thoth the very great", the Egyptian god of letters, particularly of works on astrology, magic and alchemy. He became the great mystical author for the Neo-Platonists and for all devotees of mysticism. See Milton's *Il Penseroso*, l. 88.

10*d*13 *Justus Lipsius*] Latinised name of Joest Lip, a Belgian classical scholar (1547–1606).

10*d*13–14 *Thomam illum . . . constat*] It is generally agreed that the fellow Tom Thumb was none other than Hercules.

10*d*14–15 Mr. *Midwinter*] See note on PREFACE 66–67.

10*d*17 Dr. *B——y*] Dr Bentley.

10*d*26 *The other three*] Edmund Spencer, *The Faerie Queene*, II. x. 7 and 73. Stanza 73 reads "giants killed" and not "giants had", as Fielding records it. This is probably nothing more than an error in transcription, which Fielding occasionally makes. The interesting thing about the footnotes is not the occasional error of this kind, but the care and exactness which Fielding displays.

10*d*30 Risum teneatis, Amici] May you keep back your laughter, friends.

10 Giants in *Guild-hall*] two carved and decorated giants called Gog and Magog who perched, and still perch, on pedestals above the balcony in Guild-hall (the seat of government for eighteenth-century London) except when they were paraded in the Lord Mayor's annual pageant.

18*e*1 Mr. *D——s*] Mr Dennis.

18*e*4 *Persian Princess*] Theobald, *The Persian Princess*, I. I, (p. 5).

18*e*5 *Aurengzebe*] John Dryden, *Aureng-Zebe* (London, 1676), I. I, (p. 3).

18*e*6 *Emmeline* in Dryden] John Dryden, *King Arthur: Or, The British Worthy* (London, 1691), I. I, (p. 4).

18*e*11 *or Eyes beheld*] John Banks, *Cyrus The Great: Or, The Tragedy of Love* (London, 1696), V. III, (p. 53).

18*e*12 Mr. *D——s*] Mr Dennis.

24*f*2 *Mary Q. of Scots*] John Banks, *The Albion Queens: Or, The Death of Mary, Queen of Scotland* (London, 1704), I. I, (p. 10), an alteration of his earlier play, *The Island Queens*.

26–36 Sure he was . . . take the Child away] None of these references to Thumb's begetting and size is to be found in the ballad. They were probably added by Fielding for a political satiric purpose. The audience would probably have thought of the prime minister, Sir Robert Walpole. See F. Homes Dudden, *Henry Fielding* (Oxford, 1952), I, 68.

26*g*2 Liberty Asserted] John Dennis, *Liberty Asserted* (London, 1704), I. II, (p. 9).

32*h*1 *Omne majus . . . protest*] Every greater contains a smaller within itself, but a smaller cannot contain a greater within itself.

Joseph Justus Scaliger (1540–1609), the great French classical scholar, was not the author of this axiom.

32*h*5 *Prison of thy Body*] Banks, *The Unhappy Favourite*, II. I, (p. 22).

32*h*8 Aurengzebe] Dryden, *Aureng-Zebe*, v. I, (p. 74).

34*i*3 E. of *Essex*] Banks, *The Unhappy Favourite*, III. I, (p. 36).

37*k*2 Trumpet's formal Sound] Banks, *Cyrus the Great*, III. I, (p. 25).

I. II

1*l*8 *Mistress of the Feast*] John Gay, *The Captives* (London, 1724), III. v, (p. 35).

5*m*1 Sophonisba] Thomson, *Sophonisba*, III. III, (p. 27).

5*m*2 Ibid] *Op. cit.*, v. IV, (p. 54).

5*m*4 Busiris] Edward Young, *Busiris, King of Egypt* (London, 1719), I. II, (p. 11).

8*n*2 E. of *Essex*] Banks, *The Unhappy Favourite*, III. I, (p. 34).

11*o*4 Lee's Sophonisba] Nathaniel Lee, *Sophonisba: Or, Hannibal's Overthrow* (London, 1676), III. I, (p. 27).

11*o*7 Mithridates] Nathaniel Lee, *Mithridates King of Pontus* (London, 1678), I. I, (p. 5).

11*o*10 Cyrus the Great] Banks, *Cyrus the Great*, II. I, (p. 21).

11*o*13 Royal Villain] Theobald, *The Persian Princess*, IV. III, (p. 47).

11*o*16 Anna Bullen] John Banks, *Vertue Betray'd. Or, Anne Bullen* (London, 1682), IV. I, (p. 52).

11*o*20 Cyrus the Great] Banks, *Cyrus the Great*, v. I, (p. 47).

17*p*1 Mr. *D——s*] Dennis.

17*p*4 Mithrid.] Lee, *Mithridates*, v. II, (p. 72).

17*p*8 *Was drunk*] Thomson, *Sophonisba*, III. III, (p. 29).

17*p*9 Mr. *D——s*] Dennis.

17*p*13 *drunk to Night*] Nahum Tate, *Injur'd Love: Or, The Cruel Husband* (London, 1707), I. III, (p. 14).

17*p*15 Gloriana] Nathaniel Lee, *Gloriana, Or, The Court of Augustus Caesar* (London, 1676), v. I, (p. 50).

19*q*2 Cleom.] John Dryden, *Cleomenes, The Spartan Heroe* (London, 1692), v. II, (p. 56).

I. III

1*r*2 Victim] Charles Johnson, *The Victim* (London, 1714), III. I, (p. 35).

1*r*3 Busiris] Young, *Busiris*, III. III, (p. 34).

2 Debt] The references to debt, receipts and money probably referred to Sir Robert Walpole's handling of public funds. Just as the trouble that Thumb has getting the giants within the walls of the city may refer to Walpole's difficulty in getting the city merchants willingly to accept the recently signed treaty with Spain, the Treaty of Seville.

6*t*1 *Captives*] Gay, *The Captives*, I. VII, (p. 13).

8*3 Nero] Nathaniel Lee, *The Tragedy of Nero, Emperour of Rome* (London, 1675), III. I, (p. 24).

8*4 Sebastian] Dryden, *Don Sebastian*, v. I, (p. 117).

20*x*3 Lu. Jun. Brut.] Nathaniel Lee, *Lucius Junius Brutus; Father of his Country* (London, 1681), v. I, (p. 62).

20*x*5 *This is a Man*] John Dryden and Nathaniel Lee, *The Duke of Guise* (London, 1683), I. I, (p. 10).

20*x*12 All for Love] John Dryden, *All for Love: Or, The World well Lost* (London, 1678), I. I, (p. 13).

20*x*15 *form a Statue*] Banks, *The Unhappy Favourite*, III. I, (p. 36).

26*y*1 Mr. *W——*] Hillhouse suggests that this is the minor critic-poet Leonard Welsted (1688–1747) who had quarrelled with Pope and thus found a place in *The Dunciad.* But because these footnotes seem devoted to a parody of scholarship, this might as easily be William Wotton, one of the scholars involved in the ancient and modern controversy, who had written an attack on Swift's *Tale of a Tub* and whom Swift had memorialised in footnotes when he reissued *The Tale* in 1710.

27*z*7 Man of nine] a contradiction of the Preface.

38*a*2 Mithrid] Lee, *Mithridates*, v. II, (p. 76).

38*a*3 Injur'd Love] Tate, *Injur'd Love*, v. III, (p. 69).

47*b*2 *faithful Slave*] Theobald, *The Persian Princess*, IV. I, (p. 40).

52*c*5 yon Cypress Boughs] Gay, *The Captives*, II. I, (p. 15).

57*d*2 *Love Triumphant*] John Dryden, *Love Triumphant; Or, Nature will Prevail* (London, 1694), I. I. The situation more than the speech is parodied here.

63*e*2 *Charms I lay*] Young, *The Revenge*, II. I, (p. 22).

66*g*4 *Anna Bullen*] Banks, *Vertue Betray'd*, II. I, (p. 19).

66*g*5 Cyrus the Great] Banks, *Cyrus the Great*, v. I, (p. 49).

66*g*7 D. of Guise] Dryden and Lee, *The Duke of Guise*, III. II, (p. 31).

66*g*9 New Sophonisba] Thomson, *Sophonisba*, III. II, (p. 25).

66*g*11 Ibidem] *Op. cit.*, III. III, (p. 31).

69 crack the String] This reductive metaphor of violin tuning was a favourite satiric trope in the eighteenth century. It can be found in Swift's *Tale of a Tub* (1704) and in Stern's *Tristram Shandy* (1760–67). They may have taken it from Erasmus' *Moriae encomium* or *Praise of Folly* (1511). For both Erasmus and Fielding the metaphor is certainly used to ridicule medieval pictorial cosmologies, illustrating the harmony of the spheres, in which all is drawn together by a God-held violin bow. Fielding elsewhere ridiculed these cosmologies and the poetic absurdities to which they led (see *Tragedy of Tragedies*, II. X, 1–3).

70 *Jove*] Roman father of the gods, often identified with the Greek god, Zeus.

74*h*2 New Sophonisba] *Op. cit.*, III. III, (p. 33).

79 Let *Macedonia*] Like a good satiric list, this is arranged on a diminishing scale. The King moves from heroes of antiquity (Alexander of Macedonia and the Caesars of Rome), to contemporary polite terms of address (Messieur and Mynheer), to patronymics (Os and Macs, meaning son of) to Tom Thumb. The countries also follow this same pattern — from the great classical empires, Macedonia and Rome, through continental nations, to Scotland and Ireland, to England.

88*i*1 Anna Bullen] Banks, *Vertue Betray'd*, III. I (p. 31).

89*k*3 Liberty Asserted] Dennis, *Liberty Asserted*, IV. VI, (p. 50).

91*l*2 Banks] Banks, *Vertue Betray'd*, I. II, (p. 14).

94*m*2 Albion Queens] Banks, *The Albion Queens*, II. I, (p. 20).

96*n*3 *you are mov'd*] Banks, *Cyrus the Great*, III. I, (p. 24).

I. IV

1*q*3 Essex, *&c.*] Banks, *The Unhappy Favourite*, II. I, (p. 24).

3 *Monmouth-Street*] a street on which used clothing shops were located in eighteenth-century London.

7 Saint *Paul's* Cupola] the brilliantly-

executed dome of Sir Christopher Wren's cathedral. The Wren cathedral replaced the old Saint Paul's, which was destroyed in the Great Fire in 1666. Wren's dome over an internal cupola was still, in Fielding's time, one of the architectural wonders of the age.

8 *Fleet-Ditch*] the lower reaches of the Hole Bourne river, which empties into the Thames at Fleet Lane, London. The pollution was so bad by the eighteenth century, despite several attempts to clean it up and even widen it, that it had in fact become an open sewer, into which the bank-side markets and dwellers dumped all their refuse.

I. V

1*r*1 *Earl of Essex*] Banks, *The Unhappy Favourite*, I. I, (p. 1).

5 *Billingsgate*] a City Ward bordering the Thames, famous for its fish market and for its sharp-tongued, cursing fishwives and porters.

14*s*3 *to ev'ry word*] Banks, *Cyrus the Great*, II. I, (p. 19).

17 The Hallaloo of Fire] the cry that aroused people so that they could form a bucket brigade or help pull down a burning building.

28*t*2 Mary Q. of Scots] Banks, *The Albion Queens*, V. I, (p. 62).

31*u*2 *Naval Lyrick*] a pindaric ode by Edward Young that had come out only a few days before Fielding's *Tom Thumb*.

36*x*5 State of Innocence] Dryden, *State of Innocence*, IV. I, (p. 27).

48*y*3 *this, 'tis true*] Banks, *The Unhappy Favourite*, III. I, (p. 33).

48*y*5 *that ever was*] Banks, *Cyrus the Great*, IV. I, (p. 32).

52*z*1 *Aristotle*] a bogus citation from Aristotle's *Poetics*.

52*z*7 Injur'd Love] Tate, *Injur'd Love*, I. III, (p. 11). The word play is on hawking, which can mean the sport of falconry or spitting.

I. VI

7*zz*3 *Scales of Heav'n*] Dryden, *King Arthur*, I. I, (p. 1).

7*zz*5 *in the Scales*] Dryden, *Don Sebastian*, IV. I, (p. 69).

II. I

11*a*2 Character of *Bajazet*] Rowe, *Tamerlane*, II. II, (p. 22).

II. II

7*c*6 *is thy Crime*] Dryden, *Don Sebastian*, II. I, (p. 37).

23*d*1 Mr. *D——s*] Dennis.

23*d*6 *Busiris*] Young, *Busiris*, IV. I, (p. 43).

23*d*7 Ibid] *Op. cit.* V. I, (p. 68).

23*d*10 Mary Q. of Scots] Banks, *The Albion Queens*, III. I, (p. 35).

38*e*3 Aurengzebe] Dryden, *Aureng-Zebe*, IV. I, (p. 48).

38*e*6 *the Fray's begun*] Theobald, *The Persian Princess*, V. III, (p. 54).

II. III

1*f*1 in the same Words] Dryden, *All For Love*, I. I, (p. 8).

10*g*1 Otway's Marius] Otway, *Marius*, II. II, (p. 18). Otway had, of course, borrowed this from Shakespeare's *Romeo and Juliet*, II. II.

16*h*2 Victim] Johnson, *The Victim*, I. I, (p. 5).

16*h*3 Noah's Flood] Edward Ecclestone, *Noah's Flood: Or, The History of the General Deluge* (London, 1679), I. I, (p. 5).

II. IV

4*i*5 Gloriana] Lee, *Gloriana*, II. I, (p. 14).

10 half a Pig] The Princess Huncamunca's gross appetite may be a

satiric thrust at the corpulent Princess Royal, Anne.

11*k*2 Conquest of Granada] Dryden, *The Conquest of Granada*, Part II, IV. III, (p. 132).

11*k*6 Bank's Earl of Essex] Banks, *The Unhappy Favourite*, II. I, (p. 22).

11*k*10 State of Innocence] Dryden, *The State of Innocence*, IV. II, (p. 32)

14*l*1 Mr. *D——s*] Dennis.

14*l*8 Cleomenes] Dryden, *Cleomenes*, II. II, (p. 21).

25*m*2 Lee's Sophonisba] Lee, *Sophonisba*, III. III, (p. 37).

35 lead Apes in Hell] the proverbial fate of old maids, and one facing Anne, the Princess Royal before she married the deformed Prince of Orange in 1733.

38*n*2 so great a Stroke to the late *French* King] Dennis' anti-Jacobite and anti-French sentiments were clearly known. His fear and timidity following his public statements (in his criticism and his drama) had become the joke of the town.

38*n*4 *in his Arm*] Dennis, *Liberty Asserted*, I. II, (p. 7).

38*n*5 *in her Eyes*] *Op. cit.* II. IV, (p. 23).

38*n*7 *along my Soul*] *Op. cit.* III. I, (p. 30).

42 ride Post] This originally applied to the practice of changing to fresh horses, stationed at post-inns at intervals along the road, thus carrying the mail or important passengers with the greatest possible speed from one stage to the next. Later, anyone in a hurry could ride from one post station to another for a fee.

48*o*3 Gloriana] Lee, *Gloriana*, IV. I, (p. 39).

48 Jove] Jove or Zeus or Jupiter (usually thought of as synonymous) had a number of encounters with human females. He usually assumed an animal form (a bull or a swan) for these rapes. His most famous rape produced Helen of Troy.

II. V

1*p*1 Mr. *W*——] Wotton. See comment on I. III. 26*y* above.

1*p*3 *Sophonisba*, oh] Thomson, *Sophonisba*, III. II, (p. 23).

1*p*4 *Narva*, oh] *Op. cit.*, II. III, (p. 20).

1*p*5 Duke upon Duke] a broadside ballad published in 1720, ten years before Thomson's play.

2 pouting Breasts] The references to breasts in this play may have been intended as a satiric cut at the corpulent Princess Royal, Anne.

7*3 *full of Game*] John Fletcher and Philip Massinger, *The Tragedy of Rollo Duke of Normandy* [*The Bloody Brother*] (London, 1639), V. II, (Ilr).

25*q*3 Hannibal] Lee, *Sophonisba*, V. II, (p. 60).

34 *Prussian* Grenadier] the famous tall and burly soldiers of the King of Prussia. Townshend, Secretary of State, had been buying Prussian friendship in order to protect George II's Hanover interests.

41*r*4 Albion Queens] Banks, *The Albion Queens*, II. I, (p. 14).

45 *Doctors Commons*] The college or "common house" (dissolved in 1857), provided for lawyers practising in Ecclesiastical and Admiralty courts, located between St Paul's Cathedral and the river, was a place to get a marriage license quickly.

48 the Fleet] A Fleet marriage was one performed clandestinely, without banns or license, by a disreputable clergyman either imprisoned in Fleet Street prison or

frequenting the area near the prison.

52*s*3 Hannibal] Lee, *Sophonisba*, I. I, (p. 4).

52*s*5 Duke of Guise] not the *Duke of Guise* but Lee's, *Caesar Borgia*, IV. I, (p. 47).

52*s*6 Gloriana] Lee, *Gloriana*, IV. I, (p. 36).

II. VI

3*t*3 Aurengzebe] Dryden, *Aureng-Zebe*, II. I, (p. 21).

3*t*4 Busiris] Young, *Busiris*, V. I, (p. 59).

5*u*6 State of Innocence] Dryden, *State of Innocence*, IV. II, (p. 30).

5*u*10 All for Love] Dryden, *All For Love*, III. I, (p. 42).

5*u*14 Cleomenes] Dryden, *Cleomenes*, II. II, (p. 21).

5*u*16 Sebastian] Dryden, *Don Sebastian*, II. I, (p. 26).

5*u*18 Anna Bullen] Banks, *Vertue Betray'd*, III. I, (p. 34).

5*u*22 Sebastian] Dryden, *Don Sebastian*, II. I, (p. 31).

5*u*26 King Arthur] Dryden, *King Arthur*, II. I, (p. 10).

5*u*33 *and eternal Joy*] Thomson, *Sophonisba*, I. IV, (p. 10).

6*x*1 *Anna Bullen*] Banks, *Vertue Betray'd*, I. II, (p. 7).

12*y*5 Conquest of Granada] Dryden, *The Conquest of Granada*, Part I, III. I, (p. 30).

II. VII

1*z*2–3 a Scene which Mr. *Addison* inveighs against] See *All for Love* III. I for the scene between Cleopatra and Octavia. Addison's criticism of the scene, and other extravagances in tragedy, appears in *The Guardian*, No. 110.

13*zz*1 Mr D.] Dennis.

13*zz*4 Injur'd Love] Tate, *Injur'd Love*, III. III, (p. 34).

24*a*1 Mr. *L*——] Hillhouse suggests that this may be George, first Baron Lyttleton who had recently written in fulsome praise of Pope.

24*a*7 Earl of Essex] Banks, *The Unhappy Favourite*, III. I, (p. 35).

35*b*1 Aurengzebe] Dryden, *Aureng-Zebe*, IV. I, (p. 63).

35*b*2 Cleom.] Dryden, *Cleomenes*, IV. I, (p. 44).

38*c*3 Anna Bullen] Banks, *Vertue Betray'd*, I. I, (p. 3).

38 The World's four Winds] the traditional way of thinking of the winds as issuing from the four points of the compass.

39*d*1 Verba tragica] the language of tragedy.

II. VIII

2*e*2 Love Triumph.] Dryden, *Love Triumphant*, IV. I, (p. 53).

4*f*5 Sebastian] Dryden, *Don Sebastian*, II. I, (p. 22).

7*g*2 Aurengzebe] Dryden, *Aureng-Zebe*, III. I, (p. 40).

12*i*3 Anna Bullen] Banks, *Vertue Betray'd*, II. I, (p. 19).

17*k*7 *Eurydice*] See David Mallet, *Eurydice* (London, 1731), IV. VIII, (p. 65).

17*k*9 *Statues of Despair*] Young, *Busiris*, IV, a stage direction.

17*k*10 *Curaeleves . . . stupent*] Trivial cares speak forth, but mighty ones are struck dumb. Seneca, *Phaedra*, 607.

17*k*11 *Egyptian* King in *Herodotus*] Herodutus, *Thalia*, III. 14. In defeat King Psammenitus refused to lament the troubles of his own house (his son was being led away to death and his daughter to be sold into bondage), but he did lament, the fate of an old comrade reduced to beggary.

17*k*12 the excellent *Montagne*] a

parody of Dryden's reference to Montaigne in his *Preface to the Fables*. See *Oeuvres Complètes De Montaigne*, Bk. II, Chapter II, *De La Tristesse*.

20*l*4 Don Carlos] not Don Carlos but a speech by Kitty and Filbert in I. II of Gay's burlesque of heroic drama called the *What D'Ye Call It* (London, 1715), pp. 13–14.

II. IX

7*m*2 Busiris] Young, *Busiris*, III. III, (p. 34).

7*m*3 Gloriana] Lee, *Gloriana*, III. II, (p. 29).

8*n*6 Duke of Guise] Dryden and Lee, *Duke of Guise*, II. I, (p. 15).

8*n*8 Conquest of Granada] Dryden, *The Conquest of Granada*, Part II, I. I, (p. 77).

8*n*9 Ibid] *Op. cit.*, II. I, (p. 90).

8*n*11 State of Innocence] Dryden, *The State of Innocence*, II. III, (p. 13).

8*n*14 Earl of Essex] Banks, *The Unhappy Favourite*, III. I, (p. 39).

8*n*17 Sophonisba] Thomson, *Sophonisba*, IV. IV, (p. 43).

8*n*19 Busiris] Young, *Busiris*, III. III, (p. 36).

8*n*21 Medea] Charles Johnson, *The Tragedy of Medaea* (London, 1731), I. III, (p. 12).

8*n*22 Albion Queens] Banks, *The Albion Queens*, I. I, (p. 12).

8*n*24 *assist me against me*] Dryden, *The Conquest of Granada*, Part I, II. I, (p. 18).

17*p*1 Mr. *F*——] Fielding. The Welsh were proverbially addicted to cheese.

II. X

1*q*4 Love Triumphant] Dryden, *Love Triumphant*, IV. I, (p. 52).

1*q*6 Albion Queens] Banks, *The Albion Queens*, IV. I, (p. 45).

1*q*7 *sliding off its Props*] Theobald, *The Persian Princess*, II. I,(p. 18).

1 solid Chain] the great chain of being, a metaphysical conviction that had become a poetic image by the eighteenth century. See A. O. Lovejoy's, *The Great Chain of Being* (Cambridge, Mass., 1936). A poetic and mechanistic view of the universe (often connected with the metaphysical notion of a Chain of Being as well as with the Ptolemaic universe) is also being ridiculed here by hanging the earth on axle and hinges.

8 the wonderful Bitch] as Hillhouse suggests, probably a reference to a French dog that performed (played cards if *The Grub-Street Journal* 25 Feb. 1731 is to be believed) at Drury Lane and even at Court.

10*r*2 Conq. of Granada] Dryden, *The Conquest of Granada*, Part II, IV. III, (p. 137).

13*s*1 *All for Love*] Dryden, *All for Love*, IV. I, (p. 54).

19*t*3 *Sat Majesty*] Thomson, *Sophonisba*, II. III, (p. 20).

31*u*2 Aurengzebe] Dryden, *Aureng-Zebe*, IV. I, (p. 60).

33*x*1 Aurengzebe] *Op. cit.*, IV. I, (p. 60).

39*y*1 Mr. *D*——*s*] Dennis.

39*y*5 Cyrus the Great] Banks, *Cyrus the Great*, II. I, (p. 18).

44 put into Commission] the official document by which an officer in the army or navy was appointed to the rank and command he held.

48 Willow] a symbol of grief for unrequited love.

53*z*5 Virtue Betray'd] Banks, *Vertue Betray'd*, III. I, (p. 37).

53*z*8 *Hell's empty Regions*] Theobald, *The Persian Princess*, V. III, (p. 54).

54*2 *Cato*] at the end of Act II not III of Addison's, *Cato*, p. 32.

58 thronging Vermin skreen] In the eighteenth century, bodily dirt and lice were masked by wig, powder and perfume. Few people bathed.

65†10 Conquest of Granada] Dryden, *The Conquest of Granada*, Part I, II. I, (p. 17).

65†11 My Lord *Bacon*] See *The Works of Francis Bacon*, ed. J. Spedding, R. L. Ellis, and D. D. Heath, III, Bk. I of *The Proficience and Advancement of Learning Divine and Humane*, pp. 298–299. London, 1859.

III. I

S.D. *a*2 Scarcity of Ghosts] The eighteenth century was a great age of stage machinery, and theatre managers loved to represent ghosts. For its staging of ghost scenes see Hogarth's print the *Just View of the British Stage*, or *Tom Jones*, V. XVI.

S.D. *a*8 Ψυχή . . . τραγωδίας] Plot is the soul of Tragedy. Aristotle, *Poetics*, VI. 19.

S.D. *a*8 M. *Dacier*] Andre Dacier (1651–1722) a French classical scholar.

S.D. *a*11 *Te . . . Manes*] New night will press upon you, and the fabled shades. Horace, *Odes*, I. 4. 16.

S.D. *a*15–17 *Nec quidquam . . . praetulerim*] Nor is anything in it more deserving of commendation than a certain horrifying apparition, which I should much prefer to all the other spooks (peace, Dennisisii, most learned man) with which English tragedy abounds.

3 Watchmen, whose hoarse Throats] The watchmen, who kept watch in a city ward from sunset to sunrise, cried out the hours.

6 some condemn'd to fast, some feast] another English proverb. Hell is a place of extremes; it is either "fast or feast" there. This is a variation not found in the standard dictionaries of proverbs.

III. II

5*c*3 Conq. of *Granada*] Dryden, *The Conquest of Granada*, Part I, IV. II, (p. 50).

10*d*3 so solemn an Occasion] This footnote almost exactly parallels a footnote to line 63 of Book I of Pope's *Dunciad* with notes (1729). Dennis' abhorrence for puns is mentioned. (There is a story of his leaving the company of Purcell and Congreve because of a bad pun. Fielding records Dennis' proverbial response here.) Then, Dennis' own puns are listed.

10*d*8 *must* Irene *fare*] Dennis, *Liberty Asserted*, IV. VI, (p. 49).

10*d*12 *Vows for* Greece] Johnson, *The Victim*, II. I, (p. 18).

12*e*3 Conquest of *Granada*] Dryden, *The Conquest of Granada*, Part II, IV. III, (p. 129).

12*e*4 *Cyrus* the Great] Banks, *Cyrus the Great*, II. I, (p. 20).

16*f*2 Conquest of *Granada*] Dryden, *The Conquest of Granada*, Part II, IV. III, (p. 129).

16*f*5 *I'll on*] not by King Arthur but by Oedipus in John Dryden and Nathaniel Lee's, *Oedipus* (London, 1679), II. II, (p. 29).

19 on pain of the *Red-Sea*] a folk belief that ghosts feared "drowning" in the Red Sea.

22 *Holland's* Gin] This grain spirit, flavoured with juniper berries, was originally made in Geneva (whence

it takes its name, "Geneva spirit", *i.e.* Gin) and then in Holland. In the eighteenth century, as an inexpensive, tax free, liquor, gin ravaged the lower classes of London. See Hogarth's print *Gin Lane*.

37*g*5 *Cyrus* the Great] Banks, *Cyrus the Great*, V. II, (pp. 51–2).

38*h*1 Conquest of *Granada*] Dryden, *The Conquest of Granada*, Part II, IV. III, (p. 130).

46 So have I seen] As Hillhouse points out, this is a typical introduction for elaborate Homeric similies.

49 *Pluto's* Shore] the banks of the river Styx, the river of forgetfulness, across which (according to Greek mythology) Charon conducted the dead.

58*k*5 *I know not*] Dryden, *King Arthur*, II. I, (p. 15).

60 frighted . . . by the Cocks] A ghost's activities proverbially ended with the crowing of the first cock. This might also be a parody of the ghost scene in the first act of Hamlet; Fielding has elsewhere in the play parodied Shakespeare's language.

III. IV

3*l*2 Ind. Emp.] John Dryden, *The Indian Emperor, Or, The Conquest of Mexico By the Spaniards* (London, 1667), IV. IV, (p. 51).

17*m*1 Sophonisba] Thomson, *Sophonisba*, IV. I, (p. 34).

21 *Danae*] Jove visited, and "raped", Danae in the form of a shower of gold.

22*o*1 Mr. *D*——] Dennis.

31 *Raree-Shows*] a peep show carried about in a box, into which the "customers" could look for a half-penny.

III. VI

6 Chocolate in Bed] Chocolate was becoming an extremely popular drink in eighteenth-century England. It had just been introduced at the end of the preceding century, and most of the flourishing coffee-houses in eighteenth-century London served it.

13*p*1–2 *Credat . . . Non ego*] Apelles, the Jew, may believe it, but not I. Horace, *Satires*, I. 5. 100–101.

13*p*2 Mr. D.] Dennis.

13*p*6–7 *Dryden's* Defence of his *Almanzor*] See Dryden's *Of Heroique Playes; an Essay*, prefixed to *The Conquest of Granada.*

13*p*12 Victim] Johnson, *The Victim*, IV. I, (p. 49).

14*q*1 Mr. *D.*] Dennis.

14*q*5 Love Triumphant] not *Love Triumphant* but Dryden's *King Arthur*, III. I, (p. 21)

14*q*8 Injur'd Love] Tate, *Injur'd Love* III. III, (p. 35).

14*q*11 *grinding Chains*] Thomson, *Sophonisba*, I. IV, (p. 10).

14*q*11 *blue Plagues*] *Op. cit.*, I. IV, (p. 11).

14*q*11 *white Occasions*] *Op. cit.*, IV. I, (p. 34).

14*q*13 *Beauty . . . with Spirit*] *Op. cit.*, II. III, (p. 20).

14*q*14 *In the . . . most curst*] Young, *The Revenge*, III. I, (p. 30).

III. VII

3*r*2 Conq. of *Granada*] Dryden, *The Conquest of Granada*, Part II, IV. II, (p. 126).

6*s*3 K. Arthur] Dryden, *King Arthur*, I. I, (p. 1).

10*t*3 Gloriana] Lee, *Gloriana* , II. I (p. 17).

11 *Elysian* Shades] the heaven of Greek mythology.

14*u*1 *Indian Emperor*] Dryden, *The Indian Emperor*, IV. IV, (p. 51).

III. VIII

S.D. *cum suis*] with their followers.

2*x*1 Conq. of *Gran.*] Dryden, *The Conquest of Granada*, Part II, III. I, (p. 101).

3*y*4 Female Warrior] Charles Hopkins, *Friendship Improv'd: Or, The Female Warriour* (London, 1700), II. I, (p. 12).

18*z*1 See the History . . .] This song is taken from the chap-book ballad "The Famous History of *Tom Thumb*" probably published by Edward Midwinter. See John Ashton, *Chap-Books of the Eighteenth Century* (London, 1882), p. 208.

35*a*3 *Pers.* Princess] Theobald, *The Persian Princess*, IV. I, (p. 41).

36*b*1 *outfaced my self*] Dryden, *The Conquest of Granada*, Part II, V. I, (p. 140).

36*b*2 K. *Arthur*] Dryden, *King Arthur*, III. I, (p. 26).

40*c*6 a Political Prophet] probably one more attempt to call attention to the political satire in the play. Walpole's plans to bring peace to England and to all Europe through the treaty of Seville brought him under severe attack in 1730 and again in 1731.

III. IX

2*d*1 Busiris] Young, *Busiris*, III. III, (p. 40).

3 for Liberty we fight] the rallying cry of all political opposition in the eighteenth century.

4*e*1 Mr. *D.*] Dennis.

4*e*4 Liberty asserted] Dennis, *Liberty Asserted*, II. II, (p. 18).

6*f*2 *Hannib.*] Lee, *Sophonisba*, V. I, (p. 52).

11–13 *A bloody Engagement* . . .] This stage direction is an adequate, if somewhat comic, description of many of the elaborately-staged battle scenes in the eighteenth century theatre.

19*g*7 Mem. Mandane] Young, *Busiris*, V. I, (p. 61).

31*h*6 Conquest of *Granada*] Dryden, *The Conquest of Granada*, Part II, III. I, (p. 104).

32*i*2 *to stop its way*] Dryden, *The Conquest of Granada*, Part II, V. II, (p. 146).

32*i*5 Gloriana] Lee, *Gloriana*, I. I, (p. 5).

33*k*1 Cleomenes] Dryden, *Cleomenes*, V. II, (p. 58).

34*l*2 *Fare's at Hand*] Dryden, *Don Sebastian*, IV. I, (p. 73).

37*m*2 Conquest of *Granada*] Dryden, *The Conquest of Granada*, Part II, IV. II, (p. 123).

38 To *Hampstead*, or to *Highgate*] Although now part of London, in the eighteenth century both were small village-suburbs frequented by merchants and their families, who wanted some of the advantages of the countryside.

43*n*1 Cleomenes] Dryden, *Cleomenes*, I. I, (p. 9).

44*o*2 Sebastian] Dryden, *Don Sebastian*, I. I, (p. 3).

III. X

4*p*5 Cleomenes] Dryden, *Cleomenes*, II. II, (p. 14).

12*q*5 *at my House To-morrow*] Henry Fielding, *The Coffee-House Politician* (London, 1730), V. XI, (p. 77).

17*r*2 *The British Worthy*] Dryden, *King Arthur*, III. I, (p. 21).

20s2 Cleomenes] Dryden, *Cleomenes*, I. I, (p. 8).

47t3 *them by the Great*] Dryden, *The Conquest of Granada*, Part I, II. I, (p. 14).

47t8 *as they lie*] Dryden, *Cleomenes*, V. II, (p. 69).

47t15 *I on* Angelina] John Dryden, *The Rival Ladies* (London, 1664), V. III, (p. 64).

47t27 the *French* Stage is so entirely clear] The French, like the Greeks, avoided staging acts of violence. While the results of such actions were occasionally staged, the actions themselves never were.

BIBLIOGRAPHY

ABBREVIATIONS

P.M.L.A. = *Publications of the Modern Language Association of America*
P.Q. = *Philological Quarterly*
M.L.Q. = *Modern Language Quarterly*

I. Fielding's Work

A. COMPLETE EDITIONS

Complete Works of Henry Fielding, ed. W. E. Henley. London 1903.

Until the dramatic works are issued in the Wesleyan Fielding, the W. E. Henley edition of the *Complete Works of Henry Fielding* will be the most relaible edition of his complete plays.

B. TOM THUMB *and* THE TRAGEDY OF TRAGEDIES

[Fielding, Henry.] *Tom Thumb. A Tragedy*. London 1730.

Scriblerus Secundus. *Tom Thumb. A Tragedy*. London 1730; Second Edition, London 1730; Third Edition, London 1730.

H. Scriblerus Secundus. *The Tragedy of Tragedies; or the Life and Death of Tom Thumb the Great*. London 1731; Dublin 1731; Third Edition, London 1737.

Fielding, Henry. *The Tragedy of Tragedies; or The Life and Death of Tom Thumb the Great*, ed. James T. Hillhouse. New Haven, Conn. (Yale U.P.) 1918.

II. Studies of Fielding's Work

A. GENERAL

Battestin, Martin C. *The Moral Basis of Fielding's Art*. Middletown, Conn. (Wesleyan U.P.) 1959.

Cross, W. L. *The History of Henry Fielding*. New Haven, Conn. (Yale U.P.) 1918.

Digeon, Aurélien. *The Novels of Fielding*. London (Routledge & Kegan Paul Ltd.) 1925.

Dudden, F. Homes. *Henry Fielding His Life, Works, and Times*. Oxford (Oxford U.P.) 1952.

GOGGIN, L. P. "Development of Technique in Fielding's Comedies", in *P.M.L.A.*, LXVII (1952), pp. 769–81.

GOLDEN, MORRIS. *Fielding's Moral Psychology*. Amherst (Massachusetts U.P.) 1966.

HIGHET, GILBERT. *The Anatomy of Satire*. Princeton (Princeton U.P.) 1926.

HUGHES, LEO. "The Influence of Fielding's milieu upon his humour", in *Studies in English, The University of Texas, 1944* (1945), pp. 269–97.

IRWIN, W. R. *The Making of 'Jonathan Wild'*. Reissued New York (Archer) 1966.

LOFTIS, JOHN. The *Politics of Drama in Augustan England*. Oxford (Oxford U.P.) 1963.

WRIGHT, ANDREW. *Henry Fielding: Mask and Feast*. Los Angeles and Berkeley (California U.P.) 1965.

B. TOM THUMB *and* THE TRAGEDY OF TRAGEDIES

ASHTON, JOHN. *Chap-books of the Eighteenth Century*. London 1882.

CHASE, LEWIS NATHANIEL. *The English Heroic Play*. Reissued New York (Macmillan Company) 1965.

COLEY, W. B. "Henry Fielding and the Two Walpoles", in *P.Q.*, XLV (1966), pp. 157–78.

POPE, ALEXANDER. *The Art of Sinking in Poetry*, ed. E. L. Steeves. New York (King's Crown Press) 1952.

WOODS, CHARLES. "Fielding's Epilogue for Theobald", in *P.Q.*, XXVIII (1949), pp. 419–24.

GLOSSARIES

Tom Thumb

a setting-dog — (a) *in hunting a setting as opposed to a pointing dog*, (b) *a defecating dog*, I. V. 43.
action — *legal suit*, II. II. 25.
arrack-punch (rack) — *any liqueur or cordial from the Middle-East (usually a cocoa-flavoured liqueur)*, I. II. 20.
attend — *await*, II. VI. I.

bailiff — *policeman (specifically an officer of justice under a sheriff)*, II. I. S.D.
beaus — *dandies*, EPILOGUE 6
birth-day suit — (a) *a suit of clothes, usually extremely elegant, purchased to be worn on the King's birthday*, (b) *nude*, I. I. 3.
blubber'd — (a) *swollen (or fat)*, (b) *wet with tears*, I. II. 6.
bound — *limit*, I. III. 29.
buckle — *curl*, I. VI. 4.
buskin — *the high, thick-soled boot worn in Athenian tragedy*, PREFACE 69.

catecumen — *probably from the natural chemical substance catechu used for diarrhoea*, II. VI. 5.
chairmen — *men who carried sedan chairs*, II. THE LAST. 9.
charms — (a) *indefinite attractiveness*, (b) *specific physical attributes (breasts and pudenda)*, II. II. 6.
consort — *concert*, I. III. 9.
cotemporary — (a) *contemporary*, (b) *equally fleeting or ephemeral*, PREFACE 63.
country dance — *a folk dance, most of which were danced in round or square by multiple couples*, II. IV. 23.
coxcomb — *a particularly affected dandy*, I. IV. I.

diaphormane — *fever or inflammation which arrests normal perspiration*, II. VI. 4.
distemper — *disease (thought to occur because of a disproportion in the four bodily humours)*, II. V. 14.
doctor's feather — (a) *a quill pen*, (b) *a means of confirming death. (A feather was placed on the nostrils to see whether or not there was breath enough to move it.)*, EPILOGUE 14.

eke	*besides,* II. THE LAST. 25.
epithalamium	*wedding song in praise of the bride and bridegroom,* II. XI. S.D.
gallant	*formal lover,* II. X. 5.
genius	*dominating character or spirit,* I. I. 14.
gripes	*stomach cramps,* II. VI. 8.
gudgeons	*small, sardine-like fish,* II. THE LAST. 17.
hackney-coachmen	*drivers of coaches kept for hire,* II. THE LAST. 9.
half-pay officer	*an officer temporarily not in active service because his ship or regiment is no longer in use—thus on half-pay,* II. I. 6.
hymeneal	*marriage,* I. III. 54.
links	*men who hired themselves out to conduct people along the unlit London streets with links (torches) made of tow and pitch,* II. THE LAST. 8.
musick	*musicians,* PREFACE 79.
mute	*characters without a speaking part,* PREFACE 75.
odsbobs	*a common oath with a variety of meanings, probably means God's (ods) noise (bobs),* I. V. 10.
phaenix	*the mythical desert bird which, after building its own funeral pyre, destroys itself only to rise again from its own ashes,* II. X. 2.
place	*an official function at Court. (The poet John Gay was offered the* place *of Gentleman-Usher to the two year old Princess Louisa and declined it.) Such functionaries were usually called courtiers,* EPILOGUE 15.
porters	*burden carriers who moved almost everything through the streets of London, where horse and cart were often blocked by traffic or mud,* II. THE LAST. 9.
pottle	*a large jug or basket,* II. VIII. 23.
railing	*scolding,* II. III. 33.
range	*row,* I. III. 17.
regon	*probably from regorge, to vomit,* II. VI. 5.
shoe-boys	*shoe-shine boys,* II. THE LAST. 8.
sock	*the sock or low shoe worn in Athenian comedy.* PREFACE 69.
spark	*a dandy with a pretence to wit,* EPILOGUE 17.
spunging-house	*a bailiff's house where an accused man was held pending his trial, and where the bailiff spunged (robbed) the accused by making him pay heavily for his keep,* II. I. 18.

toupees	*dandies noted for the size of their wigs. (Pope uses this as an example of metonymy in* The Art of Sinking in Poetry, *adding a footnote explaining that toupee is "a sort of Periwig: [a word] in use this present Year 1727.")*, EPILOGUE 5.
transported	*carried away with emotion*, II. VIII. 19.
witty on	*witty at the expense of*, EPILOGUE 6.
zephyr	*a poeticism for wind. Zephyrus, of course, is the West Wind, son of Astraeus and Eos and messenger of spring*, II. III. 24.

THE TRAGEDY OF TRAGEDIES

Words already glossed for *Tom Thumb* will not be glossed again.

bait	*to make a short stop for refreshments*, III. IX. 32.
battledoor	*badminton or shuttlecock racket*, II. V. 43.
bladder	*anything inflated and hollow (often a cow's stomach)*, III. II. 13.
burgomasters	*Mayors of Dutch towns*, PREFACE 18.
carper:	*a fault finder*, III. VI. 14*q*10.
confounded	*damned*, I. V. 3.
conjunction	*union*, III. X. 12*q*1.
drams	$\frac{1}{8}$ *fluid ounce (usually any small glass of spirits)*, III. IV. 8.
durgen	*a dwarf*, II. V. 19.
emblem	*symbol*, III. X. 12*q*2.
encounter with	*battle*, III. VI. 3.
fie upon you	*shame on you*, II. IX. 5.
game	*object of ridicule*, II. V. 7.
grenadiers	*originally designated grenade throwers, but by the eighteenth century it simply meant the tallest and finest men in the regiment*, I. III. 44.
half guinea	*a small gold coin whose value was established at ten shillings and sixpence in 1717, coined from Charles II reign to 1813*, II. VII. 32.
half seas over	*drunk*, I. II. 19.
joint stool	*low three-legged stool*, II. V. 32.

king of clouts	*a mere doll in the dress of a King*, I. III. 99.
lading	*load*, I. III. 39.
laid	*killed*, III. II. 21.
lightens	*grows light*, II. IV. 38.
lights	*states or conditions*, PREFACE 81.
like	*likely to be*, III. III. 2.
made a shift	*managed with difficulty*, I. III. 26.
meanness	*to be either poor or socially inferior*, II. V. 10.
mumble	*to chew or bite softly*, II. IV. 33.
odzooks	*an oath contraction of "God's succour"*, I. III. 77.
pate	*head*, III. V. 6.
physognominical	*the art of reading character from the size or shape of face or form*, PREFACE 123.
plaister	*a sticky topical medication used to heal external wounds and draw "humors" out of the body*, II. VIII. 12.
pos	*positive*, I. III. 85.
prentices	*apprentices*, II. VII. 29.
prodigious-minded	*evil-minded*, I. V. I.
promis'd	*engaged*, II. V. 18.
rise	*vomit*, III. IX. 4e5.
serene	(a) *an honorific epithet given to a reigning prince*, (b) *untroubled by thought*, III. V. I.
shuttlecock	*badminton or shuttlecock "bird" (a small piece of cork fitted with a crown of feathers)*, II. V. 44.
sit poorly down	*sit down to a simple meal*, II. VII. 16.
small shot	*a number of small pellets of lead used in a single charge*, II. IV. 40.
solecism	*a violation of the rules of grammar or syntax*, II. IX. 8*n*26.
spring	*source or origin of action*, PREFACE 100.
sprites	*ghosts*, III. IV. 4.
sure as a gun	*an English proverb meaning with absolute certainty*, III. II. 21.
the town	(a) *the London theatre audience*, (b) *the witty sophisticates of London*, PREFACE I.
truckle	*to submit timidly*, I. III. 100.
virago	*a vigorous woman, also a shrewish scold*, DRAMATIS PERSONAE 24.
wind-cholick	*the gaseousness of a sour stomach*, I. III. 54.
withal	*with*, III. VII. 3.